BITS & PIECES OF AN ORDINARY MAN'S LIFE

By Carl Fazio

Bits & Pieces of an Ordinary Man's Life

©2021 by Carl Fazio

All rights reserved. No part of this publication may be reproduced or transmitted in any form or by any means, electronic or mechanical, including photocopying, recording, or any other information storage and retrieval system, without the written permission of the publisher.

Some names have been changed to respect the privacy of people mentioned in this book.

Printed in the United States of America

Published in Hellertown, PA

ISBN 978-1-952481-26-0

Library of Congress Control Number: 2021911390

2 4 6 8 10 9 7 5 3 1 paperback

Cover design by Carla Salinsky

For information or to purchase bulk copies, contact Jennifer@BrightCommunications.net.

To my wife, Christine

I met my wife, Christine, in a night club in June of 1973. It was a warm comfortable summer night, and all the stars were in their designated positions, sparkling the evening sky. Whatever celestial influences decided our fate, we knew we'd be together for the rest of our lives. Our introductory conversation was initially comedic and casual. Little did I know that she would become the most valuable person in my (at that time) uncertain life. By February 24, 1974, in the witness of family and friends, we were married in Saint Aloysins Church in Wilkes-Barre, Pennsylvania. Our wedding song was "We've Only Just Begun." During the past 47 years of marriage, she has been everything a wife could possibly be, and more.

When we first met, some of her acquaintances warned her that I "was a womanizer, and she would be better off without me!" Her response was, "I make my own judgments." She may well have been better off without me, and perhaps enjoy a better quality of life, with some other man and going in another direction. But I would not! Christine has been the ultimate paradigm of fidelity and love for all in her family. She is the best example of integrity I have ever known. My life without her would've been an endless drift of emptiness, as it was before I met her.

She was and still is blonde, tall, slender, and gorgeous, with a cosmopolitan air of sophistication. Our first kiss under a soft lit lamppost was impossible to describe. I loved her instantly and will continue loving her into the beyond.

Whatever transcendent forces arranged our unity made me one of the luckiest men on this planet. Her instincts and wisdom have been a proven value for all throughout her professional career. As we have aged and grown in our united wisdom, the original vows of "Until death do we part" now have a more impactful meaning, as a philosophic extension of those marital vows we now have a metaphysical one, a spiritual commitment as we cross over to reside together forever.

Bits and pieces of an ordinary man's live best describes my often-disconnected thoughts and actual events that occurred during my life. I believe the whole of anyone's life cannot be summed up in anyone's environment, single event, episode, or momentary passion. Mankind is more complicated than concrete labels. Man's existence from cradle to grave is a continuum of changes both physical and mental, making adjustments along the way, and cannot effectively be described as being particularly unique!

In the interest of presenting my experiences as an ordinary man, I hope you will understand the title of this book and why I am bits and pieces of an ordinary man.

The question is: Do you pursue knowledge to add more weapons to your dark side?

Do you boastfully parade among society with false pride, while the truth you hide?

Or are you a curator of helpful ideas to improve conditions for your fellow man?

Are you realistically aware that in the spectrum of knowledge we're all innocent lambs?

My father, Paul Fazio, always said:

"If a man says he has an idea, listen.

He just might have!

If a man tells you he's sick, listen.

He just might be!"

Contents

Introduction	Page 11
Dogs Love	Page 13
Small Government, Small Minds	Page 24
My Racial Experience	Page 31
Time	Page 39
Bargain	Page 40
Seed	Page 41
One Dress	Page 43
Transgender	Page 44
Sick White	Page 46
Intellectual Cowards	Page 48
It Takes a Woman	Page 50
Flaws	Page 52
Transference	Page 53
John the Doorman	Page 55
Heroism	Page 57
Butchy	Page 58
Quiet Circles of Thought	Page 71
How I Met Captain Robert Russell	Page 74
One Hell of a Trip	Page 90
A Liar Is Born	Page 98
Moments	Page 99

Jealous	Page 100
Yin Yang	Page 103
Muddy	Page 104
Where Did You Sleep Last Night?	Page 106
Together, We'll Get Through	Page 109
Heredity	Page 111
In a Dream	Page 112
Charlottesville	Page 114
Bits and Pieces	Page 115
While Beings	Page 117
A Fool	Page 119
Poor Children	Page 120
When Killing Ends, Love Begins	Page 121
On My Parents' Time	Page 123
Unsettling	Page 125
If You Care	Page 126
Penny for Your Thoughts	Page 128
Last to Leave	Page 131
Last Journey	Page 133
Global Warming	Page 135
It's All About Honor	Page 137
The Snitch	Page 138
Relax, Old Man	Page 140
Pathos	Page 141

A Homeless Mother's Dream	Page 143
Family, First and Always	Page 145
Six Feet Away	Page 146
If You Love Me	Page 147
God's Temple	Page 148
Feeling Guilty	Page 154
A Shivering Chat	Page 156
Merely a Man	Page 158
Broken Wing	Page 159
Where Are You, Daddy?	Page 160
Twin Emotions	Page 162
A Resting Place	Page 163
What's My Name?	Page 164
Unexplained	Page 166
The Heart of a Crow	Page 168
Just Thinking	Page 169
As Clouds Pass	Page 170
Blurred	Page 172
Ascending	Page 173
Silly Old Guy	Page 175
An Ocean of Tears	Page 176
Truth on the Hoof	Page 177
Searching	Page 179
Today Is Mine; Tomorrow Is Yours	Page 181

The Non-Organ	Page 184
The Neighborhood	Page 185
Retired	Page 189
Just for Awhile	Page 191
Alone	Page 193
A Friend Flew In	Page 194
About the Author	Page 197

Introduction

From a boy to a man, I was a different soul in search of something that I could never understand, struggling to understand my feelings while deficient in words and adjectives to describe the feelings in my young heart. In my early childhood, I was impoverished, and I didn't have much of what other children had. Strangely, I didn't feel envious or underprivileged. I felt a deeper sense of inner contentment, and the warmth of the sun was always in my heart and soul! I felt an unusual presence of God and was comforted by his kindness, acts of healing, and love for the sick and poor. Because of that experience, I felt oddly grateful for being poor. In time, I came to realize that deprivation is a better preparation for the sometimes harsh realities of life.

Throughout my life, I've felt for the underprivileged, the sick, and less fortunate members of our human race. I love most animals and always treat them with kindness. Although I felt the presence of God, as I became enlightened by the reality of man's greed, his hatred, and appetite for mass murdering, I wondered, Where is my God?

As I continued my journey through life, my feeling for the poor, sick, and working man has never changed. In all of my own perceived achievements, I finally understood what it was that brought peace to my soul. Working in physical therapy, I was able at times to ease the pain of others and help victims of strokes regain a loss. At this young age of 83, I've come to realize there's much more about the world and all of its wonders to love. Hating is a waste of precious time.

When I say, "about me," it's really nothing about me; it's about all the wonderful people who allowed me to be a part of their world! I am a flawed, but happy and grateful man. Yet, I am not unwise to the true universal values we all learn to share; also, the tacit lies that we would like to believe are true, as every Christmas and Easter are laden with poignant feel-good stories, stories that in end are best preserved in faith. My flaw is pretending to keep the faith while tearfully thinking how great it would be, if only they were true. Throughout this product, you may unlock my innocence of being alive in this world of darkness and light. In the greatness of all that is, or ever was, it's not about me. It's about us.

Dog's Love

December 2, 2011

When I was 19 years old serving in the US Army in LaRochelle, France, I read a book by Col. Robert Ingersoll entitled *Man Woman and Child.*

Sasha, our Argentinian Dogo

In his magnificent book, the chapter on Love was one single paragraph. Till this day, I remain impressed by his thoughts on love. Yesterday, I was discussing a dog's love, and as a result, this writing is inspired partly by Col. Ingersoll's chapter on love.

Any attempt to explain love in general terms is almost impossible. To understand love is to completely comprehend all of the passions bestowed upon man. Love is simple, love is complex. It's both a joy and sorrow, happiness and misery, and stands alone in the universe. It is the flame that lights every star in the Milky Way. Love is the master emotion that puts joy in the human heart and in a flash takes it away.

Love is the sun's warmth and the moon's enchantment. Pleasure and pain, torture and excitement, failure and success are dependents of its influence upon all walking, swimming, flying, and crawling inhabitants of this planet. Love transcends beyond comprehension so much that it blends perfectly with hatred. Hatred happens when love is absent! Even without debate, we understand that perfect human love is at best conditional. No cell of any human body is set into motion without the prime mover being love. Love is the prologue and epilogue of all that is or will ever be! Loves takes us to war and restores peace. Love is the soldier's weapon and the poet's pen, both the answer and the contradiction of conflict. Love is blurred by all the complexities built into the developmental levels of life. Time, heredity, and environment, which are in accordance with psychology's essential ingredients of all life: when and if it happens (time), where it happens (environment), and why and how it happens (heredity). As a result, the destiny of man's love is short lived, with brief moments at best, so that the major part of relationships are devoured by each participant attempt to describe their feelings and match comparisons of devotion. Essentially, it's over when it began.

Participants, having failed to realize that it's over, spend a lifetime faking orgasms and romance. They get married and have children, build homes, buy fancy cars, take exotic vacations, throw dinner parties delighting themselves with stories of how to succeed in marriage and manage relationships.

The best thing of all happens with the animals they acquire, especially dogs. Dogs become a providence ignored. God understands the conditional basis between loving humans and the unconditional love of a dog.

God, the Creator of the universe and all living things, sent the dog to earth to teach us how to love. (I think.) We haven't learned. Instead, we go to war and use the dog to attack perceived enemies and sniff out drugs.

Successful marriages are the ones with respect and common goals born of a lasting gratitude for that brief moment when you first met. Yet, marriage somehow remains to be a great social necessity — the collagenious material that binds society together. However, if it's true love that eludes and mystifies you, I suggest you take another long look into the adoring eyes of your dog! Perfidia, pervading many relationships is an unfulfilled and insatiable greed for love, rooted in a clinical incapability of trust and search for self-validation.

Mother's Love

The preceding essay's focus is upon the conditional love of humans verses the unconditional love of a dog. To be fair, a mother's love comes close. Commonly regarded as love, a mother is intensively protective and fiercely possessive. From the cradle to the grave, as the mother holds her newborn infant to her warm breasts, love begins as a co-dependent and never loses that dependency. Often not allowing the child to go free, as well as at times a child won't free up the mother. (Possessive!)

During the course of a lifetime, a hunger for comforting love persists; without satisfaction, desperation enters the heart.

What then cannot be explained in human terms is transferred to God, in the form of religious faith. Jesus, the Son of His Father God, so believed to the extent that He loved His Father God, He was so energized with that love that He could make the blind see and the lame walk. In the end, Jesus was betrayed by Judas, one of his disciples, and Jesus was subsequently crucified. He was tortured and nailed to a cross and left for a slow, bleeding death. As He looked up to His Father God, He asked, "Why hast though forsaken me?" (to love sans love being returned is betrayal.)

The nagging complexity of love is a question of the need to be loved as to that of loving. I feel that loving without being loved is more often the case. The tacit contract of loving partners who in time perceive the lack of reciprocity leads to feelings of betrayal. The absence of complete reciprocal love is filled with hatred, and hatred is a love of hatred. If we can't have it, we hate it. Much as a picture is known to be worth a thousand words, I leave you with this mental image: a clown with a tear in his eye and an obedient dog at his side. The extreme emotions of sadness and loneliness are in the clown's single tear, yet the adoring dog is there waiting for a simple pat on the head.

Love leaves a great many humans void and empty of the ultimate experience of bi-lateral reciprocal love on earth. Frustrated with the unfulfilled need, they turn to God and the faith that heaven will deliver that which they have been deprived of here on earth. For so many, life on earth becomes an empty existence and a depressed hell! Heaven could be defined as the eternal therapeutic love. Could it be that suffering is the earthly human experience required for an entry into heaven's eternal love, in that special place wherein the man finally understands why the dog was sent to earth?

Not all angels have wings, and that is why they don't all fly.

Waiting

If all that we believe in is in the end proven untrue, and death is just that: death, at the very least it's a freedom from suffering and pain. So instead of waiting to see why not, reach for the hand whose love is in the here and now. Why not touch the hand that's in your reach? Instead of searching for a friend, be a friend. Help the sick, share the bread of this life with all of God's creatures, and if and when those pearly gates open and you do ascend, all of those family members, animals, and friend who've been waiting for you will be the ultimate amen. Meanwhile, the three most important words to speak are "I love you," and the four most important words to hear are, "I love you, too!"

God's Love Channeled Through a Dog?

On November 21, 2013, Christine and I were only five days back from a cruise in the Bahamas. We were rested and happy and planned to spend Thanksgiving Day at the casino in Mount Pocono, Pennsylvania. It was to be a holiday we'd spend together without our grandchildren. Because my son and daughter-in-law would both be off work, they had plans to spend the day with her relatives. It would all work out well and be a pleasant day for everyone.

What follows here is a true accounting of my spiritual awakening. It was 10 am when we retired for that evening of November 21st. Christine had been complaining throughout the day of an earache in her right ear. Both of us thought it was sinus-related congestion. Our instinct was to take a decongestant, which should relieve the pressure in her inner ear. She managed to take two 12-hour doses as was prescribed on the over-the-counter label. However, just prior to going to bed, she said to me, "If this isn't any better in the morning, I'm going to urgent care."

I said, "Okay, I'll go with you."

Not wanting to disturb me and uncomfortable with pain in her ear, Christine got out of bed and went into our Florida room to sleep on the couch. At 3:30 am, the telephone in our bedroom started ringing, and I awoke from a deep sleep to answer the telephone, and no one was on the line. Ten minutes later, I heard Christine going into the bathroom. I called to her, asking if she heard the telephone, wondering if she had answered before I did. She didn't answer me. She then went back to the Florida room couch to sleep.

Twenty minutes later at 4 am, our dog started barking. I wondered why the dog was barking because she never barks to go out in the middle of the night. So, I got out of bed once again and noticed that the dog was resting her head on my wife's lap. Still groggy from sleeping, I let the dog out to do her business. While watching the dog in the darkness, I realized that Christine was in a state of distressed breathing. I tried calling her name to arouse her to see if she was okay.

She opened her eyes once and asked, "Carl, what?"

Her eyes were red and glazed. That's when I became really alarmed and tried repeatedly to arouse her—without success.

My first thought was she was having a stroke. Her mother had several strokes in her sixties and now because Christine is nearly 66, I wondered, *Is heredity kicking in?*

I called my son Corey and told him to get his butt up here immediately. Our home is 17 miles away from his.) I then called for an ambulance. My thinking was that if she was having a stroke, today with advanced medicine, they could reverse the effects of a stroke if caught within four hours.

The private community security where we live were at my door within minutes to help out, and the ambulance arrived soon after. Following the usual data request, the paramedics asked me where I wanted them to take her. "Get her straight to the Lehigh Valley Hospital in Allentown," I said.

Since they are rated the number one hospital in Pennsylvania, I knew they would have all of the necessary resources available for any emergency. By 5 am, November 22, 2013, Christine was in the emergency department of Lehigh Valley Hospital.

It wasn't a stoke!

When she arrived, the ED team check all of her vitals and noted that she had a temperature of 107 degrees. They immediately cut off all of her clothing and packed her naked body in ice. While they were watching for her body temperature to reduce, a doctor came to me in the waiting room and asked for permission to perform a spinal tap so they could do a fluid analysis and help identify the cause of such a high fever.

A short time later, following the spinal tap, they informed me that my wife had meningitis and would have to be admitted into the medical intensive care unit.

While in the ICU, she was intubated for breathing and feeding and given the strongest intravenous antibiotic available, Vancomycin. That therapy continued for 14 days. Throughout the 14 days, she had a sustained elevated temperature, ranging between 103.5 to a low of 99 degrees in the early morning. It took more than 48 hours for the culture report to identify the bacterial strain as strep pneumonia. With that result, they added another antibiotic, Levequin, to her regimen.

For the entire 14 days, her arms were restrained, and she was maintained in an induced coma. Life support tubes were in every orifice of her body. Severely weakened from her illness and prolonged time in bed, 23 days later, she was discharged from Lehigh Valley Hospital and admitted to the Heinz Rehabilitation Center in Wilkes-Barre, Pennsylvania. She would therein have 10 days of physical, occupational, and speech therapy. The two weeks of tubes in her throat left her aphonic with a paralyzed vocal cord. During the ice packing of her body, her right hip and right outer ankle were both freezer-burned, resulting in a deep, open lesion of her right hip and a minor lesion of her right ankle.

On the 15th day of being hospitalized, the burn surgeon decided to operate and do a skin graft to close the open wound on her right hip. The dressing of the wound would also require follow-up nursing care at the rehab, along with additional return stints to the burn center at Lehigh Valley Hospital.

Was It a Miracle?

Christine was discharged from the Heinz Rehab with restored strength and the ability to ambulate with a cane. Although at an increased volume of whisper, her speech remains aphonic and will require outpatient speech therapy.

Considering the rapid progression of her meningitis, taking her from ambulatory at 3:30 am to being super febrile and severely incapacitated in the emergency department just 2½ hours later, some people will say the 3:30 phone call was God calling and that he started the dog barking at 4. Did God send the dog to be man's secret care giver?

It's safe to say that our dog, Sasha, saved Christine's life.

Yes, the quality of care that she received at Lehigh Valley Hospital was superb; however, if her fever was allowed to progress another several hours when I would normally get out of bed, she would be dead. Whatever the reason for her survival, the sun, moon, and stars now have a deeper spiritual meaning to me.

One month after recovering from a critical illness, Christine, her grandchildren, and Sasha were reunited to enjoy a very special love at Christmas.

Small Government, Small Minds

Why do we need government, and what does government do for the governed? It functions for the common needs of people in any location in an area of interest, first a resource, a product, or a useful discovery that brings people together. As individuals, they cannot be secure in their person or environment, and for that reason government is formed. Leadership is chosen, protection for the health, safety, and welfare of the people is established with rules, regulation, and oversight that's agreed upon. They're called laws; the enforcement and security of laws is then delegated to law enforcement agencies. In small communities, it could be in the hands of a single person, such as a part-time officer, or a full-time police force in larger cities and states. Courts are established to provide a venue for deciding the guilt or innocence of any contested violations of the law. Basically, governments provide protections and enforcement for their communities. The larger the community is in population and land mass, the more its costs are for the provisions of government.

The most politicized and least understood word in all the forms of government is socialism. Right-wing politicians promote the word as something for the masses to fear.

They say:

"Socialists are coming to take away your freedoms."

"Socialism is unpatriotic and un-American."

"Socialism will take your hard-earned money and everything you have worked for and redistribute it to lazy, unworthy welfare recipients."

"Socialists will use your tax money to provide health, safety, and welfare for illegal immigrants."

Nothing could be more intellectually dishonest than those demagogic claims. As a pseudo antidote, they spin the "small government" theory as a way to counter left-wing big government's out-of-control spending. In truth "small government" is code language for the out-of-control billionaires who want no government or any oversight and zero taxes. As an additional fear factor to gather more patriotic followers, they offer fascism as a reminder of Hitler's rise to terroristic power in Germany. Naturally, the "oh my God" people don't want that, and they follow the prophets of doom down a phony path of patriotism, never realizing or understanding that the preachers of fear are the duplicates of the devils they need you to hate.

Realistically, everything involving the formation of common groups of people into a protective society requires the sharing contribution toward the costs of their collective needs. Fundamentally, the number of people in the group determines the operation costs of service. Ergo, the larger the society is, the larger the cost becomes to provide those hierarchical services. That doesn't mean that each individual pays more; the growth is compensated for by more individuals available to pay their share of the cost. Growth and survival are calculated for by the anticipated revenues needed to service the anticipated growth. So, what happens when a right-wing conservative administration arbitrarily cuts line-item costs in institutions that provide essential services for a growing number of citizens? The impact is that more people in a growth society will be cut out of those essential services. To argue the rationale further, they cut taxes, primarily for the super wealthy, with token cuts for the diminishing "middle class." Then they sloganeer with this catch disinformation phrase, "starve the beast!" And a once great society becomes a displaced, weaker, unprotected society. Small government in a big society is the dream child for the super wealthy but cannot realistically work for the collective protectoral needs in society as a whole.

While calculating the means for servicing the growth aspects of populations, consider this fact: The population of the United States during World War II was around 150 million. Today, the US population is nearly 330 million. Seventy years later, more than twice the population to service and several more wars to pay for. It doesn't take a rocket scientist to understand that the shared cost of government needs to rise and meet its contemporary cost. If our national interests are able to survive, government's expenditures must naturally increase and not decrease as in smaller government.

In simpler terms, let's look at a small start-up business such as a local tavern. It opens its operation with 12 seats at the bar and four tables. One year later, 15 people are wanting seats at the bar and eight more tables are needed to seat diners. Does he chase the overflow out the door? Or does he expand to meet the growing business needs? The answer is or should be obvious: He expands to accommodate growth!

So, how practically is socialism then applied to a large civil functioning society? Let's for a moment look at the private corporate sector of society: insurance companies sell life, home, care, and errors and omission, and health policies to large groups of people with the concept of collectively paying for an individual's insured crisis when it occurs. The theory being that not all claims will occur at the same time, and that also is practically applied socialism! A responsible government prepares societies concerns for an insurance provider's ability to service anticipated claims by requiring adequate reserve capitalization, with sanctions for undercapitalized corporations. That's socialism! Our government understanding the potential need for disaster planning, for the possibility of massive claims during hurricanes and flood events, did so by responsibly legalizing an agency we're all familiar with called FEMA: the Federal Emergency Management Act. That is also socialism! How many thoughtful Americans would like to remove these protections? Social Security is a collective system of payroll deduction throughout a worker's viable years of employment, which then allows workers in their declining years to retire without the fear of the indignity of poverty. It's also a protection for older workers who are physically less capable of performing physical tasks as they did in their younger years. Of course, it's socialism, but it's a proactive protective need for senior citizens.

Medicare provides insurance for the elderly in a likewise system of payroll deductions during productive years. Again, this is socialist, however, both Social Security and Medicare via payroll deductions being paid for by the recipients are therefore not an entitlement; it's a collective insurance policy paid for by the beneficiaries.

All forms of government have some type of institutional socialism as part of their governance. Dictators, kings, fascists, and monarchs can't rule and control without some concessions to their citizens, and those systems will be socialistic. Monetary, military, industrial, postal, healthcare, housing transportation, and food supply are all elements of practical socialism. No form of government will last very long without some essential social systems in place.

Consider the reason the League of Nations was formed following the end of World War I. Its mission was world peace. In 1949, NATO was formed, creating a Western Alliance to protect its members from the Soviet aggression. Therein we have global socialism developing in the principal interest of peace and safety among nations. I maintain that public leaders shouldn't be running away from the misguided negative political sloganeering of socialism, but energetically towards it, armed with positive historical explanations. Socialism is not the enemy of the people; pervasive greed, corruption, and political demagogic propaganda are. Unfortunately, those who died for our collective truth are being replaced by unwitting liars.

Religious socialism: What's up with those followers of Jesus Christ? Would Jesus the Son of God denounce the varied colors of His creation? Would

Jesus be okay with racism? Would Jesus be okay with slavery? Would Jesus be okay with allowing children to starve, while watching greedy overweight people eating gourmet meals? Is their Jesus the exclusive preacher of a white man's Christianity? Are the 10 commandments to be exclusively followed among white people? What about this puritanical bullshit known as the Golden Rule, which ostensibly has been replaced by the "Fuck You, Christians!" If in fact everything Jesus proclaimed on the "Sermon on the mount" is undeniably the faith they profess, He would be appalled by their contrary discriminatory actions. There's nothing smaller than small-minded hypocrites who advocate small government. Allegedly Jesus suffered a torturous death on a cross as an offering to Father God for the sin of all men. I don't believe He sacrificed Himself exclusively for white men, do you? Perhaps this Easter Sunday when you're on your knees singing hymns, you'll honestly remember why it is that we celebrate Him.

—March 5, 2021

My Racial Experience

It was November 4, 1954, one day after my 17th birthday when I boarded a train in Wilkes-Barre, Pennsylvania, heading for Fort Dix, New Jersey. Charles Rienmiller, who also turned 17 several days ahead of me in late October, was on board with me. Together, we had been sworn in by an Army recruiting officer the day before. Because we both were under the age of consent (18), parents signed the require release document.

Both of us were drop-outs from Hazleton Senior High School. At the time, both of our families were poor, and things were tight, so the both of us were loosely supervised. Because my parents were focused on the needs of my younger siblings, and because I was the oldest male of six children, I was pretty much on my own. Most of the time, my father and mother didn't know where I was, and sometimes I would be gone for days. Although they weren't prone to overseeing my activities, although they weren't openly loving, I truly believe they cared in their own way.

One of those impromptu trips I took resulted in a serious case of my being mistaken for participating in a felony, which I didn't commit. That incident brought the city police to our door and shook up my parents. The neighbors, curious about the presence of the police at the Fazio's, had plenty to gossip about, but that's a story for another day.

Both Charles and I were troubled teenagers traveling in and out of packs with other juveniles who were headed for delinquencies with the courts. Slowly some of them were already locked up; we knew if we continued our association, our prospects for employment were poor. Also, the likelihood that we would end up in the juvenile court system was a sure thing. So, we entered into a pact to enlist in the U.S. Army on our 17th birthdays.

From Wilkes-Barre to Fort Dix by train consumed the entire day, and we finally arrived at Fort Dix about 6 pm. The thing I remember most about our arrival was the mess hall (military dining room) was closed, and we were too late for the regular mealtime. However, a sympathetic cook prepared hot dogs and beans for the three of us. (We were joined by another enlistee along the way!) That was believe it or not the first decent meal I had in a long time. In my mind, things were already looking better. I went from the youthful aberrant lifestyle of having no oversight to a completely regimented military structure. I initially liked it!

Charles and I remained together throughout our basic training and were only separated for three extended months of specialty training. Following basic training, I was sent to the Camp Gordon Military Police Academy in Augusta, Georgia. Meanwhile, Charles went on to some other military camp for his choice of training. After we completed our specialized training, we found ourselves together again at Camp Kilmer, New Jersey. There we were processed for a permanent assignment in Europe. Our luck continued, and while in Germany, we were assigned to serve our full tour of duty in France.

We traveled from Zweibruken, Germany, to our assigned destinations in France by train. During that long train ride through Germany, I remember commenting on the endless farmlands of cabbage.

In Paris, we were finally separated. Charles went to Orleans, France, and I continued on to permanent duty station in LaRochelle, France. Many years later, I saw Charles again when he appeared in my tavern. It was a hilarious reunion.

Nowhere in the city of Hazleton or any of the anthracite coal mining towns in our area do I recall ever seeing a Black person during those years. During its entire socio-economic history up until the early 90s, Hazleton was all white. Particularly during the 40s and 50s, prior to my entering the US Army, Hazleton was made up of Southern and Northern white Catholic and protestant European immigrants.

Those immigrants who were brought to the United States by corporate mine owners found their way into our city to work in the mines and all its related industries. Deceived by the unfulfilled promises of good jobs and a better quality of life than the ones they left behind; they eventually began considering themselves servants. That also is a story for another time. Anyway, for the purpose of telling this story, as a young man, I had no social exposure to Black people until I entered the military in Fort Dix, New Jersey. While I was at Fort Dix training and living integrated with Black men, it proved to be ordinary, and I got along well. Actually, I felt our goals and challenges were equally the same. Thanks, at the time to the gap in my education of American history, and President Harry Truman who courageously integrated the US military, I was innocent of the Southern racial tensions.

Through the early weeks of training in Georgia, I became friends with a Black military police cadet named Grimes, and I apologizes I don't recall his first name. In the service, it was common to call soldiers by their last names, and I guess that is why it is easier to remember them by their last names. I liked Grimes, and we spent a lot of time sharing our ideas about life and of what we were learning in our training. To be honest, I thought he was more intelligent than me, and I considered him to be a better man.

Then the day for overnight passes had arrived, and the only reasonable place for servicemen to go on a limited overnight pass was Augusta, Georgia. Augusta was a military town with all of the necessary accommodations needed for soldiers on leave. In fact, when Dwight D. Eisenhower was President, he could often be seen on television playing golf in Augusta. The Army provided routine round-the-clock bus transportation for base soldiers to go back and forth to Augusta.

With my pass in my hand, and Grimes's pass in his hand, we were deciding where to go. I looked at Grimes and said, "Let's go to a movie in Augusta."

Grimes looked a me as though I came from another planet and said, "Man, don't you know where you are? I CAN'T GO INTO TOWN WITH A WHITE MAN!"

He continued to explain to me how dangerous it would be for the two of us to be seen together in racially segregated Augusta, Georgia.

At Fort Gordon, Georgia, training was integrated, and I was used to training and socializing with Black soldiers in the fort. The impact of that incident with Grimes was my first exposure to what was happening in the South. It shocked me to realize I was not allowed to openly socialize with a man who is good enough to serve his country alongside me. I was not allowed to be seen with him in the very public we both are constitutionally by oath duty bound to protect.

For both of our safety, we didn't go into Augusta together. We continued our three months of training in Fort Gordon, and I continued my friendship with Grimes. I never stopped thinking of him as my equal, and at times my better.

I have no idea whether or not Grimes is living today, but I can only hope that the Civil Rights struggles and accomplishments of Martin Luther King Jr since that time have helped to heal the many hurts of that time. Private Grimes was a better person then than I could ever hope to be. When the WHITES ONLY signs were removed from the South, if we could go back in time, he would rightfully say to me, "Fazio, let's go to a movie in Augusta."

Ironically, while serving in LaRochelle, France, I was in a barracks with two older white soldiers from Alabama. They were James Autry and Beasley. I don't recall Beasley's first name either. Both of these men were intelligent, religious, and considered gentlemen. In our barracks, there were many whites and blacks serving together, and I don't recall any racial slurs or code language coming from Autry or

Beasley. I looked up to Autry because of his general likeable demeanor and also because he was about eight years older and wiser than me during that impressionable time in my young life. I mention that only because they were Southerners during the notorious racial tensions of the 50s. I wonder what part if any Autry and Beasley were playing during the nationally televised marches and protests in Selma, Alabama. As we later learned, many Southerners weren't full of racial hatred but were reluctant to openly side with Blacks. I'm hoping that Autry and Beasley were among the non-bigoted.

President Johnson signed the Civil Rights Act into law in 1964, making racial discrimination illegal. In 2008, the day when President Barrack Obama was elected to the Presidency of the United States, the best of America was apparently achieved. Or was it? The false notion that we were at last color blind was over. Quickly the deeply rooted racial hating bigots reared their ugly heads. It's become really clear that the struggle isn't over yet. The divide between the old school whites and the new age integrators is wider than ever. With this divide, the United is becoming the several confederacies argued against in the Federalist Papers.

Until we truly become one nation under God with liberty and justice FOR ALL, as a nation racially divided, we are a weakened nation. Another Civil

War will be far worse than a watching world can contemplate. We are flawed as the world's model democracy with unrivaled power and influence because we are skeptically perceived to be united as one. When the rest of the developing nations point to our discriminatory inconsistencies, our foreign policy obsession to sponsor democracy is seen as hypocrisy. This could all be lost because we can't live up to and honor our own constitution!

Time

Years pass along with all our yesterdays of joy or sorrows.
It's about all we're able to understand about time.
A youthful time when all thoughts were about our tomorrows.
When over picket fences we would leap, and trees we'd easily climb.
Those strong limbs, which carried our undaunted bodies around,
On monkey bar rungs, from which we effortlessly swung,
And shaking a neighbor's trees until some apples fell to the ground.
Smoking in hidden places, ignorant of damage to our lungs;
While there was only one kind of music, which we all sung.
Time was endless, and the greatness we'd achieve, to us, was real.
From all the lumps, wounds, and bruises, confident we'd quickly heal.
Looking back now, it was so long ago, and it doesn't seem real.
Time, oh wonderful time, you've passed with me.
As you know, I'm old and can no longer climb an oak tree.
Or eat those green apples, they upset my old tummy.
So! Time my wonderful friend, with a wink and a wistful smile,
I'm hoping you'll stick around awhile!

Bargain

I heard the crow cry.

Its beautiful black plumage was set upon the whitest blue sky.

The early warm spring sun showed off her ebony dress.

As she sat there crowing on that naked tree branch, I must confess:

My heart copped a plea, asking, "God, have that crow land on my head."

I promised to believe, if He'd send me that sign, I'd understand.

With that tongue in cheek plea in mind,

I raised my outstretched arm to the crowing crow and imitated her sound,

I whistled, sang, and bargained with that bird I now named Kline.

I did this for awhile, feeling much like a foolish child.

Looking away, in a flutter of my eye, she was gone, nowhere to be found.

What a great feeling, just being alive, listening to a bird sing.

On a sunny, spring day, hearing a crow, being a crow, is everything!

I heard the phone ring. I didn't really need a sign!

Seed

Was a warm May day, wherein a field down below, white lilies in chorus did grow.

Blurred artistic eyes of an awestruck guy, questioned how and why in clusters they'd grow.

In his mind, he saw a picture, as of their collective beauty as they all became one.

Curious as this man could be, he entered into the field and stood among some.

In an instinctive motion, bent down and gently plucked a single lily from the ground.

Mesmerized by the beauty in his hand, what is it about the flowering treasure he found?

As he looked above, reaching to the angel of love with the lily firmly in both his hands.

He proclaimed, "This flower has its own seed, its own soul, and grows from its own stem."

Like the green leaves and white petals spreads its precious beauty on the meadow land.

It stands in a society of single white flowers, together they're as a breathless Zen.

As he walked away, feeling a pure and clean emotion, on this May day once again,

It was clear, like in any field of flowers, or in a society of birds, cattle, and men,

They are beautiful and strong and last longer when joined together.

A glorious sight, scent of perfumed flowers, a glimpse of heaven, forever to remember.

All organized things of such rare beauty among the flowers and man, under the sun

Are safe in their collective beauty, but bouquets are arranged one by one.

—March 13, 2021

Bits & Pieces of an Ordinary Man's Life

One Dress

Sasha's wardrobe and mine, with simplicity in mind
In my closet is a varied clothing line
And every imaginable style you'll happen to find.
Sasha watches me don and doff as a daily chore,
Amused at my wanting something different to wear.
I stop what is left of my attempt at style,
And observe her cocked head, which looks like a smile.
She has every fiber of her fur in place.
She doesn't shower, brush her teeth, or wash her face.
Humans, she muses, need to change every day—such stress.
Whereas I am beautiful and have only this one dress.
As a puppy, this is the dress in which I was born.
As I grew, it grew too; it's the only one I've worn.
In the mirror, the man stares at his half-shaven face,
Ponders why a dog with only one dress has such grace.
The phone's ringing!

Transgender

He sees a butterfly floating gracefully,
And he so wants it to land on me.
In every song, he is alive in its verse.
He is the breath in a galloping horse.
He is an unsettled mare off course.
He is a man full of a father's pride,
With a searching female inside.
He is reborn in every newborn infant child.
He is the excitement in everything wild.
He wants to be strong and tall like an oak tree.
He wants to be gentle and sing tenderly.
He is everything both old and new.
He is perfidious when he's not being true.
He is the power of a swift flowing river.
When he's not a taker, he's an easy giver.
He has the beastly hunger of a stalking lion.
He has the lusty heart of a chameleon.
He pretends to be anything but a phony.
The truth is, he can't hide being lonely.
Every beautiful thing he happens to see,
When he goes, who will he be, who will he be?

He feels like all things flowering are temporary!
He is the lyrics in a song, forbidden to be sung,
Because he has two hearts, beating in one.

—March 5, 2021

Sick White

Somewhere on a street corner in America an average looking man,
Shouted comments to a passerby, "Divided we now stand!"
"Without equality a united nation cannot survive!"
"Half and half may be good for coffee, but not separate lives!'
Frozen in his place, the passerby replied,
"Mister, I'm with you. I too am tired of all the lies."
"What can we do, how do we unite and get back on track?"
"White supremacists with guns and fiery hate of the Black."
"Are powerless under the law…if we dare to fight back!"
"How do we know our enemy when masks cover their chin"
"Easy, their forehead and hands have pale white skin."
"Why, sir, are they so angry at people unlike them?"
"They fear our nation is allowing to many colors to come in!"
"How do we make them understand freedom must be shared?"
"They don't know, they don't know, and really don't care."
"What is it about being united and having national security?"
"They are united, united in their belief of their white purity."
"They have their clubs, guns, and knives and are ready to fight."
"We are on the side of what's decent, civil, and right."
"The question is, 'Will we need the same weapons in this fight?'"

The passerby shook his head, thinking, *This is too much!*
He's white, I'm white, so who's out of touch?
The passerby, now a block away, looked back and heard him say,
"Divided we now stand; we must fight the fight today!"
I see he has someone's attention.
For me, we're all Americans, and this hatred is too much tension.

—March 6, 2021

Intellectual Cowards

May 28, 2021

Following a defeated U.S. Senate vote for a Commission to investigate the January 6, 2021 Insurrection on the U.S. Capitol

A man points a gun at your body; one wrong move and you're done
Are you a situational coward, no doubt, so you elect to run!
Once safely out of the gunman's sight,
You take a deep breath, a sigh of relief, you know running was right.
So, in the analysis of the event, you wisely saved your life.
In the concurring opinion of friends, family, and loving wife.
Indeed, self-preservation at the point of a killer's gun.
If when given the opportunity, it's not cowardly to run.
An observer, pardoning himself for the interruption,
Offered a paradigm of corruption for their consideration.
To escape from the danger of a criminal's gun.
Is unlike the intellectual coward's untruthful tongue!
You, sir, were right to run from the point of a gun.
But how does a whole country run from those intellectual Republican cowards' lying tongues?

You, sir, were right and thankfully you're still alive.
I ask, of those lying 35, "How does our Democracy survive?"
Calling you "intellectual cowards" is really a generous term.
When remembering those who fought and died for our Democracy
Is what you forgot, or if you ever learned!
Particularly, as upon this Memorial Day weekend, for their loss,
Our grateful nation will mourn.
Today, as we walk away from the cemeteries, wherein all the
Brave fallen patriots lie,
Remember those 35 Senators, whose oath to protect and defend,
they knowingly betrayed.
So, look long, look hard, while you're walking away.
For in those cemeteries are those cowards, draped in phony
patriotism, who lied, murdered honor, and pride,
Disgraced our flag and buried Democracy this Remembrance Day!
While behind the "twice impeached man's" big lie they hide.
Meanwhile
A bugle is sounding Taps for our soldiers' blood on Normandy's
sand,
Honoring those true patriots who gave it all for their land.
Sleep in peace, sleep in peace, soldier boy, you once had our
backs.
Today, you were betrayed by those 35 cowards' alternative facts.

It Takes a Woman

How is it that this nation's most intellectually dishonest man controls 85 percent of America's Republican voters and all members of the Republican Congress?

Do they really believe the rambling untruths habitually vomited from the mouth of Donald Trump?

Is it possible that so many Congressmen are equally as intellectually dishonest?

Or if they are simply being politically opportunistic, and if so, what is the justification for being complicit in a dishonest man's deranged ego, an ego leading a parade to destroy our Democracy?

Why is it that U.S. Congresswoman Elizabeth Cheney is the only one who has the courage of her conviction to honor her sworn oath to protect and defend the Constitution of these United States and stand up against the proven lies?

Why does it take a woman to show her party what courage looks like?

Why, in a nation with a diminishing ability to distinguish the difference between facts and fabrication, patriotism and treason, heroism and cowardice, Democracy and Autocracy, honor and dignity, God and the devil, is a Republican-led Congress frightened by America's most "power-greedy" man, Donald Trump! Sadly, those cowardly men are standing on the shoulders of an honorable, undaunted woman like Congresswoman Liz Cheney. As much as we need a two-party system for a balance in governance, what we don't need is what the Republican party has become! If the Republican party is somehow reconstituted as a truth-based viable political asset for Democracy, it will be because of a woman like U.S. Congresswoman Liz Cheney.

If our Democracy survives today's Republican intellectual cowardice, we can thank God for the deliverance of the courageous Congresswoman Liz Cheney—an honest woman with a spine!

In fairness, the following Republican Senators demonstrated a spine and joined their Democrat colleagues in favor of a Commission to Investigate the January 6, 2021 Insurrection. They are Senator Bill Cassidy, Louisiana; Senator Susan Collins, Maine; Senator Lisa Murkowski, Alaska; Senator Rob Portman, Ohio; Senator Mitt Romney, Utah; and Senator Ben Sasse, Nebraska. The legislation failed by a vote of 54 in favor and 35 against. A 60-vote majority was needed for passage.

Flaws

On the morning mirror was a reflection of an old man's frown.
Avoiding the attempt to look again,
He looked at the wrinkled shirt on the ground.
It's when enlightenment to all that is to him came!
Each wrinkle in the old shirt was part of life's game,
And nothing is as perfect, as imperfections of reflections!
Satisfied, shaved, and groomed, in his gallery an easel waits
For the masterpiece he's going to paint.
Haunted by the mirror's daunting revelation, he's compelled
To perfect on canvas the flaws he sees in himself.
The agony of complexity consumes his inpatient soul.
When echoes of a borrowed wisdom is heard, he knows
There's no such thing as a perfect horse, with a twitched nose!
Despite all the flaws, wrinkles, and imperfections we see,
All horses, men, and trees are the beauty they're meant to be.
Suddenly, he knew there was nothing he could write or do
To improve the beautiful flaws we all view!

Transference

In his nest high up in a tall, oak tree,
He was taught to leap from limb to limb; he was happy.
In his youthful agility, he played in the forest; he was free.
Suddenly, a man swerved to the right to miss the evidence of a roadkill.
His long blood-stained bushy tail was gently fluttering in the wind,
Never again to balance his leap from limb to limb.
It was a beautiful spring day, and the sun was shining bright.
The dead squirrel, I mused survived a lingering, cold night.
Dreaming of summer warm nights, listening to calls of a whipperwill.
In its short, simple happy life it didn't know, or understand
How humans destroy the environment and everything in God's land.
The sadness struck me as I channeled the most tragic fate of all.
It labored diligently, gathering many of the fallen acorns last fall.
A harvest to withstand the hardships of winter in his oak tree nest.
Blanketed with nature's thickened hair to protect his head and chest.
His acute hearing, bright glistening eyes, and tiny beating heart,

All to dream, gather, and prepare for a chance at a new start.
To enjoy a squirrel's endless social play with his siblings and friends.
When the harshness of this winter and a car brought it all to an end.
Sadly, this squirrel will never enjoy anything ever again.
Where it's a dreamless dead carcass, gives this an ending sorrow.
Man's tragic indifference to passion with his empty smiles
No concern for this squirrel, who will never see tomorrow.
Wiping out of his head the squirrel's end-of-life scream,
It was only a squirrel, not big deal; nothing is ever what it seems.
What if its death wasn't a squirrel but an infant child?

Bits & Pieces of an Ordinary Man's Life

John the Doorman

The day's work ended, and he was on a bus returning home.
His thoughts were still on Park Avenue, where he works every day.
Although he's known by all the resident billionaires, he is alone.
They, the mega rich, dutifully behaving in their snobby way,
Would coldly say, "My bags, John, and the door, please."
The windshield wipers on the bus were whispering, *Why me?*
It was the same rhythm in his heart that cleared the driver's view.
And John felt that cadence too.
As his thoughts continued on, he wondered why they didn't care.
I'm a good Christian, polite, courteous, and always there.
Whenever they leave, I say, "Have a nice day."
It's my way!
Upon their return, I greet them pleasantly; they don't seem to care.
As my umbrella protects them from the car to the door.
It doesn't matter if it's the hot sun or if the rain pours.
Laughing and giggling as they enter the elevator to go upstairs.
I, John the unseen doorman, will now go home to my place,
Where I know someone is there who I'll embrace.
The bus door opened with a loud swishing sound.

As John got out with his two feet solidly on the ground.

He was smiling, with an even wider grin. Maybe I'll paint the town.

Christmas is coming around, and with his inside voice, he would yell.

(While waiting for that white Christmas envelope)

Wherein an annual gift of fifty dollars would be found.

I'm richer than all of you, I'm going to heaven, you're going to hell.

Well, it's a doorman's Christmas, and after all I'm only the hired help.

What a day; who am I to complain; the bus driver is a lady.

Probably underpaid!

Heroism

Bravery stated in lieu of spontaneity is an empty forecast!
Such as the absence of truth is in a song never sung.
All such bragging about the past can't last.
As told from the lips of a dreamer, who thinks he's the only one.
And never seems to awaken and see the magic of dawn.
From the unending dream, of which he alone is cast.
As an exclusive worshipped hero, when it's reality it takes
In a dose of truth, which inevitably reveals him as fake.
As it is generally and widely known,
There's only so far any bull can be thrown.

Butchy

A true story

Who was Butchy? Leon (Butchy) Mikolichick lived and spent his childhood years on Laurel Hill Road, a short residential block with one popular tavern/restaurant at the end. It is located at the foot of the Laurel Hill terrace and is the road that runs directly north off of Broad Street, on PA State Route 93. In the city of Hazelton, Broad Street geographically separates north from south, and Wyoming Street separates the west from the east.

The street with its diverse cultures was a quiet and dignified area of Hazleton. The first address to the north across the street from Laurel Hill Road is where the Hazleton State Hospital was located. Today the modernized hospital is affiliated with the Lehigh Valley Hospital in Allentown, Pennsylvania. The tavern during its heyday because of the proximity is where many of the off-duty hospital staff would frequent. Through the years, this section of the city has undergone significant landscape changes; an Elks Lodge today occupies the space of an old cinder shed, which was used by the city road crew. An old dirt pathway to the quarries became a Perkins Pancake restaurant and today is a magistrate office. In the rear is the Library Lounge, a fine dining restaurant. A motel to accommodate hospital visitors is in the same location. Directly across the street below the hospital is a Kentucky Fried Chicken, which was built on an open field where we as kids played tag football. These commercial changes mostly took place to accommodate the growing transient needs of the hospital's patients and guests. None of these changes were ever to become known by Butchy.

If Butchy would've lived beyond that fateful summer day when he was 12 years old, what would his life have been like throughout the years and today? To help you and myself understand some of the unanswerable questions, I will often need to digress to an earlier age when I had a spiritual experience. So allow me to start here with some time jumping. This story cannot have significance without reviewing in part the surviving lives of the other boys, who were not reported in the news but who actually witnessed Butchy's tragic death. As follows here, a 12-year-old friend and me at nine years old were both there. This also includes the recall of William (Wilbur) Willkie, who was invited to participate in the incident but for some reason, which he couldn't remember, was unable to participate.

Two Years Earlier

It was a beautiful, sunny, summer day in Hazleton when I was about seven years old, playing alone on the property of the Lehigh Valley Coal Company, which was located west of the east end of Broad Street. Because surface mining had dangerously damaged and scarred the environment and no other recreational facilities were available, this is where many of the east end kids would roam, swim, and play. The Lehigh Valley Railroad ran through this area of the city. Underground coal mining and surface coal mining operations surrounding the city were widespread. Underground coal mining had its own network of tunneling beneath the city and was often dangerously mined too close to the surface, which created many concerns about subsidence.

With the advent of surface mining, most areas surrounding the city were replete with black slate banks and silt dams from the Colliery Industry. Anthracite coal coming from both deep mining and open pit mining was fed into the collieries to be sized for the various domestic and foreign markets. The city residents inherited this blighted environment when the industry extracted its anthracite coal from above and below the earth's surface.

Many of the abandoned quarries filled up with water coming from the deep mines and a network of natural underground springs. Over the years, the manmade mountains made up from the earth which was dug up from the quarries eventually became patched with birch and scrub pine trees. The soil conditions for those types of vegetation was adequate.

I remember some of the hard-working men who spoke in broken English, men who worked in the mines and collaries, going into the stripping when off work to harvest coal to heat their own homes. At times, some women would also pick and crack coal. As the oldest male son, it was my duty after school and especially on Saturdays to help my father by picking and cracking at least two buckets of coal. The mornings after a rain event some old men would also comb the stripping banks for their favorite mushrooms.

Guardian Angel

Threaded throughout the black silt earth areas on the edges of town were several networks of open city sewage streams. As children we always called them "shit creeks." On this one particularly beautiful summer morning, to avoid getting my hand-me-down shoes wet, I jumped from one above water stone to another to get across the creek. Upon reaching the other side, I faced another turn in the creek and needed to locate enough stones with their surfaces out of the water to start the jumping process again. As I stood there, gazing into the running creek, observing the green slime, which seemed to rhythmically dance over the rocks with the moving flow of the water. My reflection and shadow that fell across the water also kept changing. With the rhythm of the moving water, I felt an absolute fluid calm traveling throughout my young body. As I can best remember my emotion, it was the purest and most innocent moment of my life.

I remember feeling the energy and power of the sun surging through my body, and without any sophisticated knowledge of religion or metaphysics, I felt as though God in heaven reached down to fill my young heart with a love for my life and all living things. Somehow without words, ***God was touching me and telling me that I would be safe.***

Throughout the years, I have been in situations with relationships, automobiles, motorcycles, horses, and air travel when I realized that I was fortunate to end up safe! Lately, in an attempt to rationalize the meaning of my life during those moments of reflection, challenge, uncertainly, or insecurity, I would revisit that moment. (I believe most people do this.) Most men and women question the significance of our lives: Who am I? Why am I alive? What is my purpose? Whenever I have a close call or a WOW experience, I find myself back in that spiritual moment, feeling a spiritual connection.

Superstitions

I could see the oil slick up ahead with the kind of rainbow pattern that spilled oil makes after a rain. It was a childhood fear of mine ever since I was traumatized as a nine-year-old boy, witnessing a friend being electrocuted. An oil slick reminds me of the danger of liquids with electricity. After that, my fingers crossed for good luck, I would either go around the oil slick or jump over it. If there were several slicks of oil in a row, I would repeat the jumps over and over again like in a hopscotch game. The same superstition occurred whenever I would come upon a crack in the sidewalk or in a road. It didn't matter if it would be paved with macadam or cement. A crack in pavements triggered my fears of being electrocuted or struck by lightning.

Why lightning? My mother, who was deathly afraid of lightning during a storm would close the window curtains, turn off all of the lights in the house, and then burn candles. Every time the lightning would flash across the sky, she would bless herself. My father, on the other hand, would open the front door and curse the thunder and lightning bolts. I can still hear him shouting: "Go on, roll those barrels, you bearded fuck!"

As a child, I didn't know whether I should quietly bless myself with my mother or curse the elements with my father.

Back to the point: I believed the oil slicks gave me bad luck if I stepped on them. Although I eventually understood them to be some of the common superstitions many children have, it wouldn't be until my twenties that I would outgrow them. Through my childhood, I thought it was a weakness or cowardice, and I never told anyone of my superstitions and fears.

The first time I remember being a survivor was in 1947, two years after the end of World War II. The United States and other recovering warring nations were learning how to live in peace. Most of our parents were busy earning a living, if they could find work, or working in a struggling family business to support their growing families.

My father struggled to support his wife and six children with part-time jobs for years. Because he was very handy working with concrete, he would get private jobs for chimney building, wall plastering, and sidewalk construction. He did finally get a full-time job as a fireman in one of the local industrial plants.

Butchy's parents operated a local restaurant on East Broad Street in the downtown section of Hazleton.

It had been raining heavily for several days, and the lower river towns were flooded. It was common for abandoned quarries to fill up with water during those prolonged rain events. Our local quarries owned by the Lehigh Valley Coal Company did not escape inundation during that recent rainy period. In fact, the water level in one of the quarry dams near Hazleton's Shaft Colliery rose so high that a high-tension electricity line going to the Colliery was now only a few feet from the top of the water. The power line that normally would be well above the water level in that quarry could never have been reached by anyone other than professional power plant employees. So, now there it was: An electrical power line carrying 22,000 volts of electricity with amperes enough to roast any animal or human in seconds waiting for a tragedy.

On June 9, 1947, three boys became situational friends on a raft-building project: Butchy, William Weillkie (whose family lived on the same street as Butchy's family), and me. We built the raft from leftover coal operation's wooden materials we found in the area. We planned to use the raft to float on that flooded stripping dam.

On that morning, with cloudy skies over the city of Hazleton, the long rain period had ended when we gathered at the water's edge, the site where our makeshift raft was waiting to be tested. A coal and iron cop who was on the scene chased the three of us off of the property. We complied and went to a place where we could see him leave the site.

Knowing that he was gone and the area was clear, we went back. The three of us maneuvered the raft onto the water. As we were about to board, Butchy stopped us, saying," I'm a good swimmer so let me test it first, then I'll come back for you!"

William remembers turning down Butchy's invitation to join him in testing the raft. William declined the invitation as well. He no longer remembers why, and looking back, he fears he would have been on the raft too because he was a good swimmer.

We all agreed, and Butchy, along with his 12-foot oar, set the raft afloat. As the raft drifted away from the shoreline, I remember Butchy yelling back to us that the oar couldn't reach the bottom and he couldn't control the raft.

As the raft continued drifting toward the center of the dam, Butchy reached up with his oar to stop the floating raft. When he touched the electrical power line, he was killed.

Butchy fell onto the raft with his head in the water. William and I watched him lift his head out of the water several times, not fully understanding if he was fooling around or was really hurt. When his head no longer came out of the water, we got really scared.

Thinking it was our fault, William and I ran up onto the top of the mountain behind us and prayed. From our place on the mountain, we could hear sirens and see his family and others running

down to the site. Afraid to go home, we stayed on the mountain for hours. When I finally went back to my house, coal iron detectives were waiting for me with my parents. That's when I learned that Butchy was dead.

Some 60 years later, I wonder why am I reliving this event? Could it be a healing catharsis? Perhaps as the incident left me with an intractable psychic lesion. Since Butchy's death, things both spiritual and practical always return my thoughts to that day when Butchy died.

Today, as a parent of a 28-year-old man, I wonder about the emotional trauma Butchy's mother, Sophia, and his father, Francis, along with his brother and sisters experienced. I tried imagining myself in a similar position with my only son and the depth of what I would feel if I lost him. It's ineffable! Would I have the reasoning power to go on living? I am certainly grateful I was never placed in that position.

While reading the local paper, The Plain Speaker, story about the accident, I read they labeled Skinner Schauer as "twice a hero." Certainly, I agree with that assessment. Skinner and another man, Franklin Meyers, ran to the site, stripped off their clothes, and jumped into the water. Meyers immediately started cramping and Skinner changed direction to rescue Meyers before going out to the raft in an attempt to rescue Butchy!

Skinner, although a genuine hero for his actions, wasn't the only hero that day. Leon (Butchy) Mikolichick was my hero! His decision to test the raft, without us joining him, was an honorable decision with maturity beyond any expectation of a 12-year-old boy. In my opinion, his decision that morning saved my life. He was the unsung hero that day, and only we who witnessed the incident knew.

By contrast, our decision to run up to the mountaintop to pray was hardly heroic or brave. It was a choice of a panicky pair of boys too scared to act appropriately and run for help. However, I'd like to think that time and maturity have modified that type of instinct in us.

I am truly grateful for my good life as it has evolved and for Butchy's heroic decision to test the raft alone. In that moment, he was my guardian angel. Judging from his display of courage in that moment when he decided to go it alone, whatever path of life he might have chosen, I can imagine how honorable a man he could have been. The tragic loss for his family and friends was also a loss for society.

Whereas Butchy's tragic death at the age of 12 can never be justified or rationalized beyond feel-good speculations, there was the belief that future losses of life could be avoided by citizen action. Surface and underground mining for anthracite coal was in great demand for supplying all of the United States war efforts. Because of that demand, regulatory oversight of the industry was routinely ignored. Surface mining for anthracite coal, which started in the thirties grew rapidly in the forties. It wasn't until after World War II and the Korean conflict that environmental concerns from citizens and legislators resulted in restrictive mining legislation. During 1974/5, surface mining reclamation legislation was passed in both houses of Congress but was then vetoed by President Gerald Ford. However, in 1977, a more stringent legislation from both houses of Congress was sent to President Jimmy Carter, who signed it into law on August 3, 1977.

Whereas this story is about the dangerous environment we grew up in that caused the accidental death of a child, nostalgically it should be noted that many of us have fond memories of growing up in Hazleton, which was generally a safe city. Men, women, and children could walk around anywhere without the fear of being robbed, mugged, or shot. You could sleep in your home with the windows and doors unlocked and not worry about the car you forgot to lock. When you awoke in the morning with the sunshine spreading its golden warmth upon life in Hazleton, you were blessed to be in one of the best places on this planet to live.

Bits & Pieces of an Ordinary Man's Life

Quiet Circles of Thought

As the wheels of a wagon go round and round,
As is, my heart and soul searching for that which cannot be found.
The wheel of a wagon transports a cargo of goods, supplies,
By a team of large-hoofed horses swatting flies from their eyes.
My trip, like the wagon wheel, hits ruts and bumps in the road
From worn paving or from carrying an extra heavy load.
Potholes on my journey are laden by searches for the truth or lies.
As daunting as the circles may be, it's not what I see in my third eye.
When it's suffering I see among the weak, sick, poor, and hungry,
A blurred memory, a vanished moment, it's my father I see on his knees.
He's praying, but on his wrinkled face, it's only the pain I see.
When he was unemployed, it's not knowing if he could feed his family again.
Round and round was the repeating sound as of the wheels on a train.
What was the torment, I feel, what was it, to God he was saying.
Was his heart sick because of me when a child, I always disobeyed?

Did the turning wheels in his soul remind him of his own father's pain?

Where these endless circles of his journey is where my soul is going, who knows?

Why, Daddy, were you so sad? Was it because I was bad and out of control?

The agony of circles always seems to break when I see the pain in my father's face.

As the wagon's wheels halt, mine does too, and his image is gone without a trace.

Searching for the truth before we die, having never lived, is to openly hide.

The most painful thing of all about the endless round sound is not saying goodbye!

When my dream train stops and there's no more circles going round and round,

My soul seems to rest from the moving train, and there's no longer a repetitive sound.

God, grant me the courage to thank you, thank you for my time of being alive.

If I cry, touch me with the heavenly light of your hand and quietly close my eyes.

As you kept the rhythmic music of this nocturnal dream train

wheels on the track,

Maybe I'll sleep better tonight with that circular load off my back!

How I Met Captain Robert Russell

In September 1988, I was hired by Locust Mountain Treatment Center in Shenandoah, Pennsylvania, as a recreational director. The facility's main office was in Bowling Green, Kentucky. My job was to develop a recreational program for teens under 18. It was to be a new clinical adolescent program for the facility.

It lasted about one month.

The co-mingling of adults with teens in the facility seemed to be unworkable, and the program was scrapped. I remained on staff to provide recreational activity for the adult population.

Somehow in a veil of secrecy, Locust Mountain Drug and Alcohol Treatment Center sold its business to Comprehensive Addiction Program Services (CAPS), which was based in Virginia. With new ownership, the professional staff was feeling unstable and suspicious of the change. So, they petitioned the National Labor Relations Board to hole an election to unionize. However, along with the other staff, I was retained by CAPS.

The facility had 38 beds and was operating at about 60 percent capacity. With that number of empty beds, profits were down, so they hired two outside marketers to sell our clinical program.

I was growing anxious about the future survivability of our facility operating with a low census, so I wrote a marketing strategy along with tactics to achieve a full capacity. The new CEO read my report and offered me a new position as community relations representative. The offer was generous, so I accepted it, and I joined the two other members of the team.

Together, we drew up a three-state strategy with divided districts in New York, New Jersey, and Pennsylvania. In a few months, we successfully filled the 38 beds, and the facility started operating profitably.

One day in 1990, I returned to the facility of CAPS, in Shenandoah. As the recreational director for the facility, my daytrip with the clients ended, and I was entering progress notes into individual charts. I was introduced to a newly hired primary counselor, Robert Russell.

Robert, as I recall in my first impression of him, was a charismatic man, who expressed himself in a confident manner. Although the introduction was brief, my impression of him was positive.

During the following days, everything in the clinic was running smoothly, except for some casual comments from another primary counselor, Andrew Butcher.

Andrew was a big man with a colorful demeanor, who could always make me laugh. He informed me that Mr. Russell (whom I later learned was not honorably discharged from the United States Marine Corps) was a suspect in the disappearance of his wife, Captain Shirley Russell.

The dribbles of information about Mr. Russell later became known to staff. Initially I learned he was married to a Black female, who was also a Marine Captain, who suddenly disappeared. Rumors of an investigation soon became public knowledge when the Naval Intelligence Agency came into the anthracite coal regions surrounding Mr. Russell's hometown. Their mission was to comb the coal mines, stripping banks, water dams, and landfills in an effort to locate any evidence or the missing body of Shirley. Their results failed, and no evidence of Shirley was ever found.

As time went on, the rumors settled down, and Robert was proving to be a very good primary counselor. The clients and co-counselors liked him. At that time, I was becoming very busy with developing a calendar of events for the coming month. It was part of my job to develop contracts with available surrounding institutions and gymnasiums to schedule activities for our in-house clients.

Meanwhile, most of the other staff were busy lobbying for the election of a union. It was a matter of who was for or against unionizing. Having been down that street before as a pro-active union man, I opted against. The National Labor Relations Board conducted the election, and the attempt to unionize failed.

Now that CAPS had a clinical program operating at full capacity, CAPS seized the opportunity to place the business on the market. CAPS was sold to Riverside, a Philadelphia-based addictions rehabilitation center.

Riverside streamlined their clinical program and furloughed most of the staff, including all three marketers. During the furlough, CAPS treated me fairly well with a generous severance package, and I soon settled into the empty but leisurely life of being unemployed. With another chapter in my life closed, I was still an elected borough mayor, so I turned my main interest back to community affairs and politics.

In the spring of 1990, I was settling into my community role as mayor, and gradually drug and alcohol rehabilitation was fading from my daily lexicon. I received a telephone call from Robert Russell, who wanted to meet me to discuss a business proposition. I was curious, so I agreed to meet him for lunch in a restaurant in Sheppton, Pennsylvania. It was the only restaurant between Hazleton and Shenandoah, a small place serving good food where I usually stopped for breakfast on my way to Shenandoah in the morning.

I don't recall the exact day, but my memory tells me it was a sunny day, and both of us were in an upbeat mood. We discussed the dynamics of treatment for addicted at length before Robert made his pitch. He suggested that because both of us had experience in the D/A field and were now unemployed, why not start our own drug and alcohol rehab center. He explained he was reaching out to me because I was experienced as a community relations representative and would be able to handle census-building for a proposed facility. He further indicated that my combined experience as a recreational director and clinical experience would be a plus. He added that my politics would also be an asset, while his clinical background experience would enable him to be the clinical director and supervise all treatment programs. Between the two of us, in his opinion, we had all of the essential ingredients necessary for business management.

I was impressed by his positive attitude and told him I would think about his business idea and let him know. Entering into a new business while still owning a town tavern with a license in safe keeping had to be weighed into my decision.

During that period of time, there wasn't any public news considering his missing wife, and I had no reason to add any suspicion to a quiet situation. He was dynamic, experienced, and intelligent, and he had a master's degree. Personally, my hunger for a new business adventure was open. So, in the following days, I had a lot to think about.

Several days passed, and I weighted the pros and cons of going into business with charismatic Robert Russell. I thought the idea was great. Human resources (us) were formidable, and all that was missing was the most important ingredient of all: capitalization! All things considered, I thought it could be a good thing having our own facility to do great things helping restore sobriety to addicted members of our society.

Meanwhile, talk of Robert's missing wife had died down, and I felt comfortable that's all it ever was: talk. After all, CAPS hied him as a professional counselor, and they must have checked all of his references before they hired him, right? And like me, he wasn't fired but furloughed due to the sale of the facility. With his certifications and counseling experience, I had no reason to believe he wouldn't be a credible business partner.

Robert called me a days later and asked if I thought about his proposal. I said that I did and was ready to discuss the logistics needed to bring the idea to reality. So, we met again at the same restaurant to identify the following steps:

- Capitol backing and finances to include all overhead and staffing costs
- Location of a facility
- Zoning and community acceptance (possible hearings)
- Client capacity
- Licensing and permits
- A brochure development to include a clinical and nutritional outline plan, with a prospectus for backers and a mission statement
- Staff recruitment

Because Robert had no personal bankroll to contribute, and I wasn't willing to invest any of my own liquid assets, we agreed to pursue financial backing. Before me was a man with a fertile idea but an empty wallet. Always cautious of being conned, my instincts wouldn't allow risking any of my hard-earned cash to go into a pot without any matched equity from a potential partner. Although the idea seemed okay, it would be a matter of how and where to reach potential backers.

We agreed that the first thing we had to do was locate a community with a suitable building for a drug and alcohol rehabilitation facility. We met again and started our search, which led us to Nesquehoning, Pennsylvania. We found a secluded orange brick mansion on a large, fenced lot, which was for sale. Following a tour of the building, we agreed this would be a wonderfully serene environment for the treatment of recovering addicts. It had everything we would need to house and treat 17 clients. We photographed the potential facility and left the community in an upbeat mood.

I agreed to develop a brochure as a prospectus with the proposed facility photos included. I developed a draft brochure and went over it with Robert. He liked it and gave it his approval. We thought recruitment of staff would be no problem because of the other laid-off counselors and support staff we had worked with. Licensing and permits with the Department of Public Welfare would be initiated and handled by Robert. With these steps completed, we were ready for the most important step of all: acquiring financial backing.

We concluded that a good place to start our search for capitol would be with the Better Business Bureau in the Wilkes University in Wilkes-Barre, Pennsylvania. While conferencing at the BBB, we learned of a venture capital venue held at the Allentown/Bethlehem Airport, a weekly luncheon meeting called the "Two Minute Forum." That luncheon provided any seekers for financial backing to give a two-minute speech detailing their business proposal.

It was an awesome experience to see a gathering of mega wealthy people in one room exhibiting capitalism at work. Every table in the room was filled with venture capitalists looking for more-than-average returns on their investments.

I was elected to give the two-minute speech. Just prior, we each had a drink. Robert had a rum and Coke, and I noticed him getting a little manic. He went into an arrogant form of laughter, which surprised me. His usual demeanor of professionalism momentarily disappeared, and he suddenly seemed common.

We survived the Two-Minute Forum and went into "wait and see" mode. Several weeks passed without hearing of any interest from the capitalist, so we were at an impasse.

While nothing significant was happening with our business proposal, Robert invited me to dinner at his home in Mahanoy City. He was living there with his new girlfriend, Susan, and her son. My wife, Christine, and I joined them for dinner. With generalized discussions and no shop talk, the dinner was friendly and pleasant. Robert, an avid deer and turkey hunter, would go into graphic details about hunting. Before we left, he gave us a frozen package of ground venison. Back at home, Christine and I placed the ground venison in our freezer and forgot about it. Within a week, we reciprocated and had Robert, Susan, and her son over for dinner at our home in Beaver Meadow.

Time passed, nothing more was happening with the business, and I didn't hear anything from Robert. One day, I received an excited telephone call from him. He informed me that he was hired by the Caron Foundation in Wernersville, Pennsylvania, as a clinical director for their newly constructed adolescent treatment center. The center was being prepared for its opening, and they were in need of an admissions counselor. He asked me if I would accept the position.

"I have no experience as an admissions counselor," I replied, shocked.

"That would be no problem. I would arrange for you to have a quick study," he replied.

I agreed, and off to Wernersville I went, where I was provided with two offices in this new facility.

Things went well at Caron, and I actually counseled the first 12 adolescent clients into treatment. Doing well, the Caron Foundation gave me a $5,000 increase in salary. That salary increase was on a Monday.

It was early Wednesday morning. While in my office, I routinely called home where my mother-in-law babysat my son, Corey. As usual, I was checking to see if everything was okay. But instead of my mother-in-law answering, my son answered the phone. I asked him to get Granny on the phone.

"She's sleeping," he said.
I felt that something was wrong, so I questioned him further and asked him to get her on the phone again.

"She's still sleeping and won't get up," he said.

"Corey, just stay by Granny and don't leave her," I said, worried.

My job was 2½ hours away, while my wife's place of employment was only 30 minutes away. I called my wife and explained what took place during the call and suggested she get home immediately. She did and at home discovered that her mother was having a stroke. I also left Wernersville after confirming that Christine would also be going home.

With my mother-in-law no longer available to take care of Corey during the day, we were faced with the choice of either giving up my new position at Caron or having my wife give up her employment with the commonwealth. Because the commonwealth was more stable and my wife had a lot of years already invested with the state, I gave up the admissions counselor position with Caron. Management at Caron couldn't believe that I would give up the job when just two days prior they gave me a $5,000 raise.

Time passed again, Robert remained at Caron, and I was back operating my night business, the Rustic Tavern in Beaver Meadows, Pennsylvania. During the day, I was able to take care of my son. In the evening, Christine would be available to help with the business and care for our son.

It wasn't too long after I left Caron that I heard again from Robert. He asked how things were going with my situation and then informed me that he also was no longer at the Caron Foundation. He was now working for the Pennsylvania Department of Corrections at Grateford as a drug and alcohol counselor. Everyone who knew anything about Pennsylvania's prisons knew that Grateford Prison was one of the worst jails in Pennsylvania. He was attending the academy as required for all corrections personnel no matter what their positions are. I explained how I was doing and wished him well with his new position.

Irony insufficiently describes what happens next.

I took the civil service test for the Department of Corrections, scored well, and was hired as a corrections officer at age 52. I didn't believe they would actually hire me at that age, but they did. So, off to the academy in Camp Hill I went for five weeks of training. It wasn't bad, but one thing that I learned in the academy was that the average life expectancy of a corrections officer is 57. I double wowed myself with the prospect of only having a few more years left.

I thought it was amazing how Robert and my paths kept crossing. While life was routinely going on as a corrections officer in the Frackville Prison, the news broke about a drug and alcohol counselor at the Grateford Prison removed from the facility by the FBI in handcuffs!

It was Robert Russell, indicted for the murder of his wife.

My first thought was that they'll never convict him without finding her body. The most compelling circumstantial evidence the prosecution presented was from a floppy disk on which he outlined 26 steps to murder your wife.

His alibi was that he was writing a novel! The jury was not convinced. Robert was convicted, and he is serving a life sentence in a federal prison.

One evening, Christine and I defrosted the ground venison that Robert gave us while at dinner with him in Mahanoy City. We made a meatloaf of it. We were enjoying its unusually good taste when suddenly we both stopped, looked at one another, and asked, "Oh, my God, you don't suppose?"

We stopped eating and discarded the rest of the meal.

I am so grateful that our attempts to start our own drug and alcohol rehab business failed. I'm very glad that I didn't put my own money into the business proposal. If we would have succeeded, I would have wound up without a partner and with all of the financial liability. Also, I'd endure the tainted responsibility that the facility was owned by a murderer. As it turned out, there were a lot of things about Robert that I didn't know about.

In conclusion, all of the potentially negative situations I have been in during my lifetime leave me with little doubt that I have a guardian angel!

For all the facts about Marine Captain Robert Russell's trial and conviction for the murder of his wife, Marine Captain Shirley Gibbs Russell, see the 1997 USA movie A Perfect Crime. On May 15, 1991, it was a feature story on local channel 28 *A Current Affair*. His conviction and sentence were in many national newspapers as well as the June 4, 1991, tabloid editions of *Globe* and *Star*.

Here is the list of 26 items as found on the floppy disk that led to his conviction:

1. Leave Thursday, 14 January 88 for Paris Island.
2. Allow 12 hours (drive).
3. Arrive at night-hide truck.
4. Check on weight of cinder block.
5. Check on anesthesia.
6. What to do with body.
7. Call Nora approx. 60 minutes from Paris Island.
8. Alibi excuse from work.
9. Cash check based on figures for gas etc.
10. Write a nice letter and mail it on Thursday.
11. Allow 2 hours return and arrive on Friday 15 January morning.
12. Pick up two checks up at the house.
13. Make it look like she left.
14. Pack suitcase and jewelry.
15. How do I kill her???
16. Buy a pair of rubber gloves and regular gloves.
17. Vacuum floor and tidy up a bit.
18. Check on a bicycle.

19. Make sure car seems to have had problems.
20. Rehearse
21. Buy some No-Doze.
22. No cologne.
23. No mask-plastic bag over feet.
24. Wash tarp!! – I may need to cut it??
25. Check on library on ways of murder-electrocution??
26. Where do I park car—blame it on her own kind.

In as much as my association with Robert Russel was professional and business related, during that time I had no reason to suspect that he was a murderer, with the exception of that one moment during our Two-Minute Forum, when he displayed a hebephrenic tendency! However, given the list on the floppy disc, itemizing his method of killing her, I would be satisfied the "Mens Rea"(intent) under the law, and if I were on the jury during his trial, I also would have voted to convict.

One Hell of a Trip

It was a cold, snowy January of 1952. The streets were plowed, and the sidewalks of Hazleton were hand shoveled  clear, except for some slippery spots. The streets and sidewalks on both sides of Broad Street had snow piled around five feet high. We kids had fun walking on the top of these snow piles.

People during those years were generally less dependent on weather forecasts to determine if schools, factories, stores, and events should be cancelled. Most everything moved by cars with chains and warmly dressed pedestrians. Whatever weather conditions were visited upon them, they dealt without panic buying, food stocking, and material hoarding that we see today.

The city of Hazleton on a cold winter night was intoxicating in my young eyes. There I was, a six-foot-two-inch tall, 14-year-old, weighing around 120 pounds. (A blooming ectomorph!?) Tall and skinny with dark Elvis Presley-looking hair and a comb in my pocket to keep each hair in place. Donning Wrangle jeans, a winter jacket, and engineer boots, which was the style of footwear for male teenagers for that time. (I probably stole the jacket.) Despite the January cold, I refused ever to wear a hat, which would spoil my combed hair.

Coming from a large family, oversight of my comings and goings was nonexistent. Accustomed to doing whatever I wanted and going wherever I pleased, I was an emancipated child long before it became fashionable as in today's progressive society.

On this one particular evening, I was unwittingly headed toward a journey leading to events I'll never forget.

Traveling from the east on Broad Street in Hazleton was the main shopping thoroughfare on route 93 to West Hazleton. We usually referred to Broad Street as going downtown. From Poplar to Boundry Street is where Hazleton ends and West Hazleton begins. On both sides of Broad Street was a spectacle replete with retail stores, bars, and restaurants. Between Cedar and Pine Streets on one side was Jimmie's Restaurant, famous for its delicious 15-cent hotdogs and 10-cent coffee. It was somewhat of a precursor of fast-food restaurants.

The hotdogs flew fast and furious at Jimmie's, and chef Leo's white apron bore the mustard and ketchup stains to prove it. It wasn't a place for kids to just hang out. Jimmie's never changed and remains open to this day, except for Tuesdays.

Directly across the street from Jimmie's was the Tip Top Restaurant, which was a place where teenagers would sip on fountain cokes and maybe have a burger. Often, I would meet my first girlfriend (JR) there and sit in a booth holding hands. When we felt that no one was looking, we'd sneak in a kiss!

On the corner of Cedar and Broad Streets was a gas station owned and operated by Packy DeVecco. Packy's as we called it, was a place where some teenaged boys fascinated with cars would hang out. I'm tempted to inject a story about a boy and a girl getting it on while hoisted inside a car on the oil-change racks—perhaps for another time! Packy was a very popular and accommodating guy!

Across the street on the opposite corner was the United States Post Office. The significance of the post office and its role in my unforgettable journey will soon be understood. Two teenagers, 16-year-old Art "Trigger" Sachs and his 17-year-old friend whose first and last name I don't recall hung out at Packy's. They were the two key actors in an event that was later revealed to me by the Hazleton City Police.

Out the door from 545 East Mine Street, I went, taking the long, brisk winter walk to the Tip Top

Restaurant on Broad Street. While listening to the crunching sounds my engineer boots were making on the frozen snow, I could see through Jimmie's frosted window, where Leo was ceremoniously preparing hotdogs. The light from the Tip Top was pouring out into the winter night. It was a warming sight for my anxious young heart. Arriving, I entered, crossing my arms and slapping both shoulders, instinctively attempting to warm my chilled body.

Inside the restaurant, a few customers were seated at the counter. In the far corner, sitting in a booth, Art and his friend were in a deep conversation. Art turned to see who just entered the restaurant. Because I was already acquainted with him through another pal of mine (Robert Craigle), he motioned for me to join them. Without any knowledge of their planning, I saw with them and engaged in small talk.

While Art's friend was and still remains to be obscure in my memory, Art "Trigger" is vivid in my memory. He was a very handsome teenager. Visualize the distinct good looks of the young movie actor Earl Flynn, with his pencil-thin mustache.

Following our initial chit-chat, they informed me that they were driving up to Rochester, New York, to see someone and asked if I wanted to go along for the ride. With having nothing else to do, I went along. And what a ride it turned out to be!

The two conspirators (Trigger and his friend, who I will from here on fictitiously refer to as John) and I left the restaurant and got into a black Plymouth sedan. John sat behind the wheel, Trigger sat in the passenger's seat, and I sat in the rear. With John driving, we were off on the 245-mile round trip to Rochester. The trip went well, and we never got lost, considering those were days without GPS. Because most of the driving was done throughout the night, passing snowbanks along sides of the highway and snow-covered rooftops in the towns, we only had one incident when our car slipped off the road into a snowbank. John managed to back out onto the road, and we continued on to Rochester. The two guys apparently were prepared with food. They had drinks, stick pepperoni, and Italian bread. We ripped into the bread and ate bite for bite of bread and pepperoni. It was an Italian feast, with small talk during the rest of the trip.

While in Rochester, John took us to a restaurant where Trigger and I were seated in a booth. John was engaged in conversation with what appeared to be a familiar waitress. While leaning into one another over the counter, they appeared to be having an intimate conversation.

I learned the waitress had worked at the Tip Top Restaurant in Hazleton and became John's girlfriend. She had left Hazleton for Rochester, maybe to get away from John, or maybe with the promise of him joining her later. Of course, I can only speculate on the reason, but in retrospect his demeanor at the time appeared worried.

John's conversation with the waitress ended, and we left the restaurant and headed back to Hazleton. Only 125 more January miles back. The trip back to Hazleton was without incident and eerily quiet. In all, the trip lasted three days. During the time I was gone, none of my family, particularly not my parents, knew where I was.

Back home, I entered the house and was greeted by my father.

"Where the fuck were you? The police are looking for you," he angrily asked.

"Why the hell would they be looking for me?" I wondered, dismissively.

I was thoroughly exhausted and desperately wanted to go to bed. I went upstairs and plopped into the bed I normally shared with my brother Thomas. In a few moments, I was fast asleep.

I wasn't home very long when the Hazleton City Police were knocking on our front door. My father answered, and the police wanted to know if I was home.

"He's in bed," my father replied,

"Get him up! We need to question him!" the police said.

Dog tired, hungry, and confused, I greeted them at the door where they took me into custody, drove to city hall, and place me in a cell behind the desk sergeant.

I knew my equally confused had to explain about what he didn't know to our relatives next door and the other neighbors of the four-row block houses where we lived.

In a state of compound youthful innocence, I was in a jail cell, not knowing what I did and what to do about what I didn't know. Somewhere in my subliminal vault, I reasoned that I should be allowed to make a phone call. Not knowing or able to afford a lawyer, I called my maybe-still girlfriend JR. I don't recall her response, but I'm guessing it wasn't good.

While I was sitting in the jail cell, the police paraded an elderly man by my cell. He nodded yes, positively identifying me as one of the thieves!

Wow! Wow! Wow was my reaction when the police informed me that the night janitor at the post office identified me as one of the guys who robbed Packy DeVecco's gas station. I sat in disbelief.

Meanwhile, the police had Trigger and John in custody for questioning, and they also impounded the Plymouth sedan. During the interrogation they searched the vehicle. Finally, Trigger and John confessed to the crime and explained that I had nothing to do with the robbery. When the police released me, they explained that Trigger and John robbed the gas station prior to going to the Tip Top Restaurant and while planning their trip, I came along and was invited to join them. They told me how lucky I was because under the rear seat where I sat was a case of dynamite and several handguns.

How much time Trigger and John did is not in my memory bank. However, Trigger went on to serve his country in the United States Air Force and also lead a productive life as a civilian. He passed away last year in his eighties. Wherever John wound up, I don't know. But I'm guessing it wasn't good.

JR married and so did I. During our first marriages, we relived our intimacies many times in secret.

A Liar is Born

The festive Christmas season had finally passed,
And back to school he was, with the rich students in his class.
There-in a negative lesson a young child in school would learn,
From an ignorant teacher, a liar would soon be born.
In the season of giving gifts in celebration of a birth,
An innocent poor boy sits impoverished in self-worth,
As requested, stood and lied of gifts he never gave or got.
It became easier as time passed, and he couldn't stop.
Nor did he ever forget the moment he fibbed,
To a first-
grade class, full of rich kids
Or a teacher who lost the moment to explain
How and why Jesus died on a cross in agonizing pain!

Moments

Moments of time in all eternity is the sum of life.

Billions of moments, each separate and different,

All seeking their own special deep meaning to survive.

Every moment of the whole assumes its unique existence.

The magical dimension is the color of those moments,

Black, white, brown, and yellow et al, must not be dread.

No easy answers, no revelations, no secrets, nothing to regret.

All saved by the beauty and wonder of being able to forget.

And appreciating that in the end, all blood is red!

—March 16, 2021

Jealous

Chomping at the bit to enlighten myself about a thing called jealousy,
What does it mean in the end, which will ultimately define treachery?
Could it be your neighbor's wife was a tantalizing tan beauty by the pool?
Was it a tendency to scoff at the education of others, making you the fool?
While on the journey to discover your purpose, it's only sorrow you found.
Every denial in your lexicon about social values was anything but sound.
As years pass, are you more about enjoying everyone else's achievements,
While hiding in the darkness of secrecy, to justify your own mal content?
As the sun casts a heartwarming shadow over the trickling stream,
A lily and narcissus adoring of the only image they're seeing,
Spend their entire lives believing they alone are the only beautiful things.

As in the harshness of ensuing winters and rainy springs, this is true.
It's easier to deny all the social rules apply to everyone else except you.
While lilies and narcissus flowers continued to bloom, wither, and die,
Others like roses, carnations, and the delicate orchids do in jealousy cry.
Does the homeless, hungry feline outside covet the warmth of the dog inside?
When, if, and ever do the twin emotions of envy and jealousy collide?
Avarice, envy, jealousy, and greed are the untamed weeds in our brains.
Like the timothy hay, flowers, trees, and grass are fertilized by the rain,
End with fresh lilies in cemeteries on the graves where all the jealous are lain.

Yin Yang

He sees a butterfly floating like in a gospel hymn.
Hopefully, he so desperately wanted it to land on him.
The rhyming in every song, he feels alive in the verse.
He is the power and oxygen fueling a galloping horse.
She is the hidden and unsettled golden mare, off course.
He is gendered as a man, full of his father's glory and pride,
Who knows nothing of his tortured son's searching female inside.
He longingly is reborn whole in every newborn infant child.
Together they wonder why they are the excitement in everything wild.
He wants to be strong and tall like a tall, full-grown, red oak tree.
She antagonistically wants to be gentle as she sings alto tenderly.
Overtly, when together they are everything both old and new,
He is secretly gay and perfidious when he's not being true.
She is the dynamic power of a swift flowing river.
When he's not being a taker, she's a flirtatious open giver.
He has the beastly hunger of a hunter stalking a lion.
She has the lusty heart of a deceptive chameleon.
He pretends to be a genuine strong man, but he's really a phony.
The only real truth is they both can't hide being lonely.
Every beautiful thing they happen to feel is the key.

The end, they muse, change is on the way when they'll be free!
He feels like all things blooming are slow at getting done!
She is singing the lyrics in a forbidden song never to be sung.
Because it appears, they do have two hearts beating in one!

Muddy

What is this thing I hear, "world without end?"
As a mother walks away from the grave of her child,
It will be a long time again before she smiles.
How and why did the red get on the rose?
Why do cat's eyes glow in the darkness of night?
Are the twinkly stars really winking at the moon,
When back on earth, a loved one is gone too soon?
Why seasons change and the sun is always there,
Why an ordinary man of ignorance, wonder, and care,
Why is it that muddy streets never bothered me
Or powerful minds brazened and made me feel free?
Like the holes in my jeans, I think were taunting poverty,
Being young, being defiant, and full of energy.
Did you know sweet elderberries grew on a bush just for me?
As a poor boy, I sucked them from their stems greedily!
Muddy streets never bothered me, until they did!
I never cared about what others thought of me, until I did.
What is different about me I can't see in other men?
What do they feel when depression and sadness happen?
Above the honking geese are turning; they stopped honking.
Once, I weakened and shared all my secrets with someone.

Except some were too shameful; they must forever stay hid.

Why muddy streets never bothered me, until they did.

There were some I walked upon, and on others I slid.

When I see someone staring at me, I wonder what I did.

Is it my hidden, dark, evil soul they think they see?

If you believe my wildness has betrayed every one of you.

Because those muddy streets never bothered me.

Well, I'm older, and like many things, now they do!

I am the street's muddy body.

God, I miss elderberries.

Where Did You Sleep Last Night?

When everything you hear forebodes another dangerous cold night,
White is everywhere in sight, the snow is piled high and packed tight.
It's a February winter reclaiming its seasonal right.
Huddled inside, quarantined families are reading Covid news by candlelight.
Their fuel is running dangerously low, and there's no place for them to go.
Hungry, their food shelves are bare, with crying babies who need their care.
The rent and utility bills are past due; an eviction notice will soon become true.
A frosted window, an ocean of white, and all the social hurt is in plain view.
Hungry babies, overwhelmed mothers, unemployed fathers, a maddening nightmare,
A Republican party, detached from the reality of poor people, don't give a damn or care!

Homeless families out of food, money, and work are in the streets in mass.
In defiance, but in compliance, six feet apart, are wearing used face masks,
Skeleton, dark, sunken-eyed victims of a bewildered, indolent, deceitful government,
Reside on sidewalks in the plain view of a disinterested privileged class.
Their whiteness is pale and threatened by the other colors pursuing freedom,
And their passion to keep what's always been exclusively theirs in the past,
Must never be shared with the unentitled, undeserving immigrants amass.
While their white eyes are vacant and their hearts are inclined to be greedy,
They're absent when it comes to loving, caring, sharing, or feeding the needy.
Mom's twirling her wedding ring, thinking hopefully of the coming spring,
When maybe God will enter all their dark hearts and change everything.

Perhaps, when the horrible stench and all the bodies are removed from sight,
The sun will shine in an attempt to disinfect and remove the blight.
White will go away, and the beautiful other colors will define a new day,
And all those cardboard boxes won't be places for the homeless to sleep.
They'll become inexpensive places for children to play.
Mom will still pause for a moment and remember those days without pain,
When truth was valued, sacred, and lies weren't alternative facts,
Those vaguely remembered days when neighbors had one another's backs.
As a tear falls while she's thinking of people loving people once again,
Forgetting how people died, with swollen bellies from a virus and malnutrition
In a lonely quarantined prison.

—February 23, 2021

Together, We'll Get Through

What does it mean to be optimistic in a land of quarantine?
What does it mean to be lonely for loved ones, never again to be seen?
Maybe optimism is a key feature for all those who made it through.
What of the one-quarter million whose final "love you" came from a window?
What are the penalties for the liars who held back the truth?
What are the sanctions for the leaders who denied the scientific proof?
What will be tomorrow's normal, with Mommy or Daddy's hand?
Why is it so difficult for our President to be honest with his fellow man?
Why did Grandpa and Grandma need to wait too long for the shot? Pass on?
If in the beginning, doing it right wouldn't have caused so many wrongs?
Together we'll make it through! On TV came, "Breaking news just in!"
Maybe it's true, but Richard's children and wife are no longer with him!

Covid cases in our US are over 2,600,000 today.

As denying, ignorant people are aiding the virus to have its way.

Heredity

Forty years and many miles away,
An unusual smile and swagger in her gait,
Why am I like this, what's in my DNA?
Who or what determined my life's fate?
Cleaning incessantly, everything must be in its place,
Who is it that gave me this pleasant face?
Why in a vision of an illusion dream
Am I haunted by a face I've never seen?
On stage singing, old songs and loving the curious are,
Where did it all come from? How did it all start?
Why are my hands also talking as I speak?
Where did it come from? Why the dimples in my cheeks?
Somewhere there is a river raging with my heredity,
Out there somewhere is my reality.
Until our rivers, if ever do meet, I'll clear my plate,
Look for someone like me in towns and crowds,
And wait, and wait, hoping it's not too late
To be wowed.

—February 27, 2021

In a Dream

In a dream, I walked through a door and entered.
It wasn't day; it wasn't night.
It wasn't dark; it wasn't light.
As real, as in his life, I recall him to be.
There stood my father, in the center.
I rushed to hug him, and he spoke nothing to me.
As dreams go, it's difficult to remember!
There were others in the room busying about,
I called upon them to "say hello to my father."
Repeatedly announcing his presence, I had to shout.
Not a person there seemed to care or be bothered.
Infuriated by their discourtesy and rudeness in a way,
Acting as though he wasn't there or hear me say,
"Say hello to my dad!"
My dream ended; his soul visited me in this dream I had,
It was Father's Day you see!
Of course, they couldn't see him; it was just a dream.
I was his soul still alive or was this his gift to me!
Or so it seemed!

Paul Fazio, my father, approximately age 20, in U.S. Army Uniform

Charlottesville

Angered, I am watching, full of passion and desire,
As hatred and racism is an out-of-control fire.
A viewer paralyzed, wondering when it will all stop.
So close in 1965 to a cure, and now so far from the top.
Distant echoes from yesterday's tortured souls, I hear,
Oddly not in screams but out of their shame and fear.
Slaves were singing songs appealing for intervention.
They are praying to God for mercy and interception.
Yet, from a faraway God, there come no answers,
As the haters, hatred, is cruel, swift, and spreads like cancer.
Close your eyes White man, pray that this isn't true,
But remember, when they're finished suppressing the Blacks,
It won't be long until they'll be coming after you!
Will you be white enough for them, to distract?

Bits and Pieces

There is a trail of bits and pieces in the life I'm leaving behind,
Bella figlia mia, take my hand, walk with me, and there you'll find,
The color of my heaven and the sounds of a thousand violins.
You'll see you in me, that adorable smile with a devilish grin.
Don't let go until you're sure you know you are where I've been.
When in time, all those fragments are woven into a whole,
There, as vivid as can be for all to see, will be our kindred soul.
Our hooded, piercing eyes, which harmlessly and openly tantalize,
Are designed to charm its prey without your pretense or disguise.
Our fragments and pieces of a heart seeking a life of love,
Scattered everywhere, always searching below and above.
Many empty days and lonely nights were always found,
Although my seeds were planted in cities and towns.
Some were special, while others were inebriated clowns.
A few friends but many acquaintances were made.
As time showed its ugly face, the year showed my age.
All those fragments and tiny pieces of love, I see in you!
And then came a special moment, what I found true.
Bella figlia mia, walk with me, and hold my trembling hand.
I'm hearing echoes of you, singing love songs in a small band.
When all the scattered fragments are assembled into a whole,

There's one thing that rings clear, it's of the human soul.
Except in the dreamer's dream, nothing is what it seems.
Walk with me, just for now, and hold my trembling hand,
And think of life's bits and pieces when you sing with the band.
It's never easy to let go, when you finally know
You're bits and pieces of my whole!

While Being

Some things are worth remembering,
Like the sunrise teasing the scents of autumn and spring.
Guiding our heartbeats through the works of a wonderful day,
Euphoric when the ending exceeds a simple okay.
With your shadow behind you, a crimson sunset is in your view,
Awesome as awesome can be, is this privileged sight you see.
Breathtakingly poignant, you sigh, is this beauty really true?
Shrugging, has God provided this vision just for me?
Some wonderful events are worth remembering,
As the thrill and excitement of watching a child grow,
When he/she has their first steps in a foot of snow.
The sounds of angelic voices singing ethereal lullabies.
The vision of her young face and pathos in their eyes,
Like the flower through the winter that has survived.
Ah, then it portends, life as beautiful as God has decreed,
No one transcends the swamps and daunting weeds,
Yet, there are always some things worth remembering.
As the snow is covering the innocent November ground,
And all the warmth, those pleasures in life you have found.
When comes the time, you will last close your eyes,
And ascend ever so gently to the waiting heavenly skies,

The warmth of your arms holding me in a warm embrace,
Remembering I was just a simple man in this human race,
Christine, with the eternal memory of your adorable face.

A Fool

And now to the external image I seemed to portray,
At this moment, this precise time, on this epic day.
My internal ID, well buried and so well hid,
Unsuppressed by the thought of pending demise,
Finally, by the limits of time does now realize,
Those thoughtless deeds were nothing but cruel,
It wasn't those of you, but I who was a fool!
I sang love songs to myself that no one heard,
As I cursed others and called them nerds.
So, to all who were victims of my external flaws,
I now confess, it wasn't you. I broke the social laws.
Am I ready for the nothingness of before I was me?
Yes! But what of all those who were the tools,
To believe I was a fool?

Poor Children

One block away from poverty street is the wealthy street.
What a difference there is between the people of their soft lights,
Hungrily seen by children on poverty street at night.
Wherein the cold, huddled children near a candle's glow,
Dream of the day when they won't be hungry and so cold.
They listen closely as the mother reads her Holy Bible,
Relating stories of Jesus and His loyal disciples.
Their pondering how wonderful it would now to be fed,
When Jesus, for all to eat, split and multiplied one loaf of bread.
She tells them how a rich man has as much of a chance,
Going to heaven as a camel has getting through the eye of a needle.
In their bedroom, shivering without heat,
Asleep, three in a bed, side by side, their tiny hearts beat.
Three dreaming in one bed all through the cold night,
Of tomorrow, when God will warm them, and all will be right.
Mother listens to their breathing in her room nearby,
So as not to be heard, she quietly cries.

When Killing Ends, Love Begins

Disappear into empty whispers, and the void is nothingness.
As is the life of a man who remains silent.
A man whose death ends sans witness that he ever was,
And now, it's my time to confess.
I do love the Creator of the universe, our Creator,
The Architect of it all, who is the space and planetary Dictator,
So much so that its transcendence silences its mystery,
While I cannot betray God's love, when to my dog I wink and smile,
Every man, woman, and child, crafted with such perfect design.
The beauty of a fawn, the agility of a squirrel and how their fur shines,
The souring magnificence of an eagle in its graceful flight.
When the rain pours, the wind blows to dry the windowpane,
Followed by a warm sun that gives me hope again.
And out of the wet forest comes to me a beautiful doe,
Trusts my outstretches hand, then kisses my nose.
I felt God's love. My heart was full and cleansed of sin!
I'll never kill a dear again or eat venison.

On My Parents' Time

While at perfect peace and calm, suddenly
A moment of midnight silence enters my thoughts,
And, as a single tear of mine hides in the darkness of this night,
Like magic, I become sadly aware of racism and bigotry.
The special moment when my mother and father fell in love,
My soul was there—vicariously. I suppose I'm right.
My heart shares their moment as I feel what they must have felt:
Prejudice, fear of community rejection or family acceptance.
A Protestant woman and a Catholic man had to be rejected,
While secretly embraced in each other's arms. The power of their kisses
Overpowered their fears of social damnation by their fellow man,
And defeated the bigot's plan!
Having no money or a place to call home, did they have a chance?
While ignoring poverty and the bigots, they continued their romance.
One year later, a girlchild was born. Another year, a son!
So, that's why I'm here, dancing their dance and smiling their smile.
I'm singing in my heart—all their old love songs,
Wondering, as their marriage lasted long, was society so wrong?

I'm walking in their time and in their shoes.
Call it melancholy, whatever you choose, as I sing the blues.
I cry, hoping they went to their deserved home up above.
The son of their son has two daughters, who never knew
What bigotry and hate were like and what their grandparents in love went through.
As I analyze the why and how it all must have been,
My midnight, watery eyes are for the powerful love they were in.
While ending this vicarious moment of midnight drama,
I turn now to this divisive, national moment we're in and ask,
Why, with all the majestic beauty I see, it's always of my momma?
Let's pretend God has a challenge for all the souls of children and men,
To end the bigot's hateful control of tomorrow's endless, stained traumas.

Unsettling

Waking from a confusing dream, he was enraged,
Unable to control the residual feelings, he set the stage.
An untenable thought pervades through his being.
Why this lingering rage? Whatever does it mean?
No balance of a tortured mind was he able to find.
The whys were unending; they just kept coming.
To what could he compare? What would settle his mind?
In a mirror, he was bent to stare at his tired, vacant eyes.
Still, he believed there was some truth to be realized.
He sensed he would need to send his soul on a mission,
To a place where his rage matched his own dark vision.
The dark waters of the North Atlantic Ocean tides,
Where angry waves smash ships against wharfs that cried.
I am dark, ugly, and mad. Everything I am not makes me sad.
When I'm not enraged and hating, I am gentle and loving.
Not softened by the tender thought of being in many loves,
From the mirror he turns with outstretched arms, looking above,
"How, dear God? How can I love so many equally apart?
So why, dear God, have You given me only one heart?"
Tonight, maybe I'll dream again, this time of tranquility,
And the peaceful waters of Hawaii.

If You Care

On the stage stood an old, white-haired sage,
Speaking to a corporate audience, lending their ears,
But not really caring to accept what they were about to hear,
About the injustice plaguing the underpaid worker's wage,
Likening the plight of the coal mine mules, who never understood or knew
The loads they were carrying were full of valued black jewels.
He admonished the poets to think before they use their pen and ink,
Not to prostitute the importance or the cost of writing before you think.
"Write on, write on of the pathetic amount you may have paid,
Remembering this: Nothing's ever cheaper than have a slave."
To the artists, he cautioned, "It's the difference of what you see
In the end that determines what's meant to be
On your canvas that will last an eternity."
To all the angelic voices on high who sing,
He imputes this one and only thing:
"Sing on, sing on to the poor, hungry, and lonely.
Sing for their hearts and their tears only."
I say to all of you, "Do all the good that you might.

Keep faith with your fellow man, then all will be right.
Walk every day with love of your privileged being.
When in the pure hands of angels, cross over to that night,
Into the world of eternal, heavenly light."
And with that the aging sage, having nothing more to say,
Bowed and humbled, left the stage.
Outside, the early evening was muggy and hot.
As he walked, screaming sirens were racing to the spot
Where a gathering crowd looked at a Black boy who was shot!
Walking home to an empty house, the old man shrugged.
An empty house, no one there—what he needed now was a hug!
What fool thinks his passions are the passions of others?
Except for all those grieving mothers!

Penny for Your Thoughts

In a house of siblings, poor with meager means,
There lived an adorably little girl with nothing but her dreams.
Although thin and gangly as a child, at times teasingly wild,
She was the sweetest little thing, everyone could see,
Growing up in a town close to me.
Her hair was black with a sheen like the feathers of a crow.
Her eyes sparkled like black diamonds in fresh snow.
Her smile was coquettish, and on her friends, it would grow.
Her heart was open and full of all the wonders of life.
At night, she'd dream of someday being a mother and wife.
Her children wouldn't go to bed hungry and sob themselves to sleep.
Their father they would know; it's a promise she would keep.
There were times while walking to and from school,
She would ask herself about the father she never knew.
A lover of the arts, whose tiny heart like the perfume of a morning dew,
She could sing and paint and make simple things beautiful.
She was bubbly and mostly liked by the people she met,
Yet this haunting feeling of being illegitimate wouldn't go away,
What was her secret? Would it eventually be gone one day?

The years sped by and gone were the days of nickels and dimes.
With all her inherent talents, she thrived and shined.
This girl, with an obsession to achieve bachelor's and master's degrees
In the arts, she would always move to the head of her class
And identified with the loneliness of Wyeth's girl in the grass.
Maturing into a proud, sensitive woman, all of the world could see:
Life and things happened as she went from town to town,
Always focused on what was important and still looking around,
Hoping one day, there would be no more secret holding her head down.
At times, she would still paint and sing love songs.
Her tiny heart grew larger, caring about the poor and social wrongs.
Remembering always her days of nickels and dimes, she went along.
Then kismet, life's door, opened, and it was her saint she met.
That's the way her Tom came along.
Together, they became their own love song.
Everyone in their orbit listened as she sang and he played a guitar,
Songs of the heart were their repertoire.

Long since forgotten were the days of nickels and dimes,
When in her arms, she held the shiniest little Penny.
Her raven hair, devilish eyes, and adorable smile,
Happiest she'd ever been, would confide in a friend,
Soon she felt her secret would end!
It was a glorious sunny summer day of 2020,
When on a park bench, she first found the face always blurred.
It was his, but more importantly hers.
Today, she's forty. In her heart is Mom, Tom, and Penny,
A true love story of two who are three with glowing pride,
As on sunny days, bicycles they'd ride,
Remembering always
On a day in 2020, when her sadness went away.
Happy birthday!

Bits & Pieces of an Ordinary Man's Life

Last to Leave

As darkness slowly swept upon the November sky,
In a window, an orange light appeared, a silhouette was seen.
It was a nightly thing for an elderly guy.
Below, under a lamppost, stood a curious man pondering why,
Who thought intently about this motionless being.
What was he thinking? What was he dreaming?
Was life in the dark street a reminder of his passing years?
Were thoughts of his life after death something near?
Were the silhouettes of his wife and children long gone?
Could it be he was just listening to old songs?
Maybe he just wanted to hear the life sounds from the street.
Did he have years, months, or days until God he'd meet?
As the curious guy under the lamppost started to depart,
Thinking, "I guess he's just an old, lonely heart."
Looking back for one last glance, the window was black.
The silhouette was, too. Why ever did he look back?
Tomorrow's nocturnal November sky
Will be much colder in December when he remembers
The orange light and the silhouette that's gone forever,
As the lamppost man realizes to his surprise,
It was all about thoughts of his own demise!

As he thought of the lonely silhouette in the window,
It was really of him in the nocturnal orange glow.

Last Journey

Ever so gently floating, ascending, spiritually floating,
As of a white feather on a soft cloud, I am at peace.
That love song without words I've always heard
Was never silenced, never hated—only love was in my heart—
Sings on in this world to silence greed and hatred.
In understanding the why, acts of kindness,
Old movies, and yesterday's lovers, tears fill my eyes.
In this thing about us as living humans
Craves the arcane evidence of life in our world:
To feel the sun's warmth, moonlight magic, the stars bright
As diamonds beautifying the darkest night.
Music, flowers, and animals feeding our hearts and souls,
Only then to be sadly slaughtered.
Upon this gentle cloud, there's no torture or pain; all's healed
To love and be loved in memory.
Ever so peacefully, I am floating on a spiritual cloud,
Leaving this place I love to a promise of heavenly love above,
Ascending, never ending, never ending, never ending...
Until I'm gone, gone from here. And then, as if I never was.
As though nothing ever existed,
Until I was here with you, then we, then family.

Then to understand it's only being alive,
Therein is the only proof of a world that ever was.
On this beautiful, soft cloud, I gently ride to the end,
Gazing about this solemn place to see family and friends.
For all those whose love delivered my body and my soul
Unto the universe of heaven and its eternal peace.
There then, I'll wait for the softest and purest white cloud
To deliver all the humans, cats, dogs, horses, and deer,
All the loves of my life, to share within this new heaven.
Where together, all of us will reside in a lasting peace,
Resting, all of us together on the purest white cloud,
Where the music of angels goes on forever.

Global Warming

Once upon a time, a long, long time ago,
There was no time, or time as we have come to know.
Timekeepers didn't exist, there was nothing but a vast endless space.
Nothing eclipsed anything, not even a human race.
All was darkness, broken by glimmering stars and comets to trace.
And then the moons, sun, and bright stars were joined with a new face
By the appearance of a planet Earth in that once timeless, quiet space.
Among all the stars in the universe, spinning ever so quietly,
Around a sun on a peaceful journey, now with a living society,
When somehow, sustained life in many forms began to appear.
Man as the master species of all, dominated with power and fear.
He invented time; the minute, the hour, week, month, and year.
And to remain dominant, it somehow became a vital necessity
For spiders to eat flies, and tigers and lions to eat deer,
And as man needed to have power over all life's territory,
He ate the flesh and consumed all the inferior life forms.
Fearful of losing a single thing, even a worm,

He imprisoned, then destroyed, all opposition.
Spears to arrows, rifles replaced bows; It was about ammunition.
Cannons, guns, all man's weapons were ready and loaded.
Bigger and more destructive bombs were being exploded.
Single homicides became mass Christian crusade executions,
And in the name of God, it was justified religious genocide.
Behind the colorful robes and jeweled crowns, King would hide.
Greed, disguised as "National Interest," replaced patriotism.
Armies of loyal subjects formed and obediently fought the King's mission.
Man's wars progressed to bombs and bullets, ripping at the planet's skin,
And man's appetite has the ozone layer growing dangerously thin.
Ice caps melting more each year with an ocean being warmed,
Native Americans and scientists were sounding the growing alarms.
It became harder to breathe, water too poisoned to drink.
All living things unable to breathe, eat, or drink will become extinct.
What's left of planet Earth will be reclaimed by the silent universe.
Without man and his invention of time, of course,
As a star, it might once again have a new birth.

It's All About Honor

Courage is the willingness to suffer the consequence of a conviction!

There exists no advance determination of when your time will arise.

For courage, there is no prediction.

Cowardly as anyone may be, the moment of truth will be a surprise.

Inside every inner man, a deceitful coward hides.

Inside the same man, a situational hero resides.

When conflicting emotions emerge, the truth will decide:

Does the hero conquer the coward's lies?

An anxious nation waits for the 45 U.S. Republican senators

Whose cowardly political party's only motive is to survive.

Citizens torn between a cult of destruction and habitual lies,

Do they succumb to treason or act with honor and pride?

With a nation's democracy now at stake,

For democracy to survive, how much fact and truth will it take?

The Snitch

Evil pen, in the darkness you hide,
So full of hatred, but so empty of pride.
Before you judge anyone to be wrong,
Make sure you're right.
The twins of argument are always brought along
With honorable, civil compromise in sight!
And if evil was unable to honorably ascribe,
You'll find in the shadows of darkness, a coward hides.
He'll use a poisonous pen to create a plan
To destroy the love between child, woman, and man.
With evil intent, whose ego was hopelessly inspired,
Frustrated and angry, lost is all when it backfired.
What they sought to destroy wasn't very clever.
The love they wished to destroy is stronger than ever.
So, to you, I say, Mary, John, Joe, Paul, or Jay,
"Anonymity is a game anyone can play."
If you're listening, Nancy, Alice, or Howard,
Perhaps it's you who is the spineless coward?
For your superior intellect, I'm enclosing these for you,
And I sincerely hope they'll do:
You can pick 'em.

If you find ones you like, you know where to stick 'em!

This is a hint for you who think you know,

"Be careful when trying to screw with a Scorpio!"

Relax, Old Man

He was all set to go; his lungs were filled to capacity.
Upon a new road, his rich red blood is charged with fresh audacity.
Idling in place, waiting for the gun shot to start the race,
To higher heights, where every heart and mind finds a better place.
Slinking and snaking around his cranium lurks a new project,
Wherein maybe, just maybe, he'll develop a stronger rocket.
Let me see now, to continue on with this cryptic metaphor,
I'll cut off the rusty hinges on that old subliminal vault door,
To peek inside and see what nuances are waiting to emerge.
And, wow! Nothing is there; nothing he hasn't seen before.
Like an old, dusty room, all that useless rust must be purged.
Well, anyway, he tried. Now it's time to deflate and exhale.
Being all set to go is nothing new for a dreamer's unlit torch,
Who spends hours on a broken swing, on his broken down porch.
Maybe tomorrow there'll be fresh inspiration to hit the trail.
Satisfied, with his alibies being justified,
Tomorrow, he really must find someone to bring him his mail!

Pathos

Is your soul in your eyes and your heart in your hands?
If it is so, you are so welcome to all the inhabitants of this land.
Pathos, kindness, loving, and being loved, are the best of man!
When your soul is in your eyes, and your heart is in your hands,
Those you see and touch spread tranquility among your fellow man.
The space between agony and ecstasy is in the depth of your reach,
And the sincerity of the healing is chambered in the breach.
On a gentle, dancing twig sits a tanager in its full, red-feathered dress.
Without knowledge of the rhythm of its self-beating heart, sheds happiness.
To everyone in view, its perfect soul is in its eyes,
Its heart is its wing spread, and oh, how gracefully it flies.
And predictably returns from its mission with worms and butterflies,
To nourish the waiting chicks and end their hungry cries.
Where is your heart and where is your soul?
Where have you been and where will you go?
When you're there, will you know?

Are you aware that in the eyes of your soul, cataracts will soon grow?
Your heart will need to remember the love you did once sow!
Chicks are huddled in snow covered branches of an evergreen spruce,
Night has darkened as the tanager returned to his nest.
Silently with his chicks, contented, through the night he rests.
Quietly, a complete heart and soul is a natural, feathered truth.

Scarlet Tanager

A Homeless Mother's Dream

Tough time for everyone, says the man turning his thermostat to seventy,
Then opened the door of his refrigerator with food aplenty,
She, half awake and half asleep, rolls over for another forty winks,
While their spoiled daughter brushes her teeth and doesn't clean the sink.
Outside, noises infiltrate from the early morning street.
The morning news warns of keeping a safe distance from people they meet.
Later, at the breakfast table with their smart phones, they sit,
Stuffing their mouths with lots of foods while complaining of getting too fat.
With a few precious moments to spare before going out the door,
The mother hauntingly mentions her dream that they were poor.
Suddenly, honking horns and distance voiced she hears as she tried to wake.
She felt the hard city sidewalk where she fell asleep next to a grate.
It was a dream! A dream of a homeless woman who lost it all!

Cold, hungry, and in miserable pain, she didn't have a single Tylenol!
Her husband, she recalls, was in prison for stealing food in a shopping mall;
Her only daughter long gone, hadn't been heard of since last fall.
As tough and impossible as it may seem for those like us who once had it all,
It was quickly taken away by the banks in a few swift days.
Alone, cold on a city sidewalk with nothing to eat or drink, too weak to pray,
All she had left that they couldn't take away were her dreams of yesterday.
From a distance, she heard someone say, "Happy Mother's Day!"
It was for people to keep their social distance from the likes of she,
She was a mother! A homeless mother! As homeless as anyone could be.
In her dream, she was all alone on a cold sidewalk in abject poverty!

Family First and Always

We were young once and had so many friends.
They're all gone now, and it's only family that matters in the end.
We were all about having fun then and playing in the street,
Day and night, out of sight to avoid our parents' calls for retreat.
We were young, we were young with lots of friends;
But it's only family that mattered in the end.
When our same-age friends came around to play,
Younger siblings weren't always welcome, they'd be in the way.
We'd make lame excuses and threats to make them go away,
Promising to have fun together—some other day!
We were young, we were young with lots of friends;
But it's always family that matters in the end.
The time will come when our life's journey is through,
And all of those you know won't be there to say goodbye to me or you.
It's not a cry for what or where you've been in the past;
We all know childhood friendships rarely ever last.
We were young, we were young with lots of friends;
But it's always family that matters in the end.

Bits & Pieces of an Ordinary Man's Life

Six Feet Away

It's the right thing to do,
You stay away from me, and I'll stay away from you.
I'll cover my face, if you do too,
It will show you care as much as I care for you.
And if everyone understands it is the right way,
The day will come again when we'll all be okay,
And no longer need to be six feet away.
It's the right thing to do,
You stay away from me, and I'll stay away from you.
I'll cover my face, if you do too?
For now, holding each other's hand is the wrong thing to do.
We all must think this terrible disease through.
It's not because I don't love you; it's the right thing to do.
Because this Corona virus is not the usual type of flu.
The day will come when family, neighbors, and friends,
Unmasked will be back hand in hand once again,
And the social distancing required today will end,
If everyone does their share and show they care.
Stop saying, "Social distancing and wearing masks isn't fair."
For now, it's the right thing to do if you care.
If we all do, it's really saying, "I truly do love you!"

If You Love Me

A Song

Please tell me that you hate me and wish me dead.

It would hurt a lot less than the bits of love I'm being fed.

Show me the indifference, it's easier to function with instead.

Let me get back to the me without you in my head.

It's only because of a love that can never be sustained,

When in its absence causes debilitating pain.

It's hard to get back to a normal life as distant friends.

Please tell me you hate me and never want to see me again.

If you love me, hate me; it's better in the end.

God's Temple

It's now mid-morning, December 2nd, 2015, and it's 23 days before Christmas. My arthritic fingers are painfully eager to dance upon this neglected, dusty old keyboard. As eager as I am to put something in print, what I feel unable to deal with are many of the disturbing subjects that cannot, and never will be, unveiled. To see what cannot be seen, or to attempt to answer the unanswerable questions about God. In my opinion, however, one word about religion says it all, and the word is "faith!" Faith and loyalty without evidence is the explained, celebrated wisdom of its followers. However, a great deal more must be offered by anyone who tries explaining faith, while at the same time, no utterance from mortal lips will ever satisfy that which transcends the mental capability of the human mind. Oh, what a wonderful world it would be if only it was true. Our galaxy of breathtakingly brilliant stars majestically residing in an organized solar system so clear to the naked eye from the planet Earth on a clear night magnifies the vast mystery of the human existence.

Christmas Eve mass was poignant, and as usual, I sat teary-eyed, while the story about the birth of Jesus Christ was allegorically presented at an improvised manger by children, acting in the roles of angels and shepherds. My tears were not of confirmation for what the salvation of his birth represents, but for what a wonderful world it would be—If only it was all true!

It's been my observation through the years that people of all faiths generally will seek answers to validate their existence on this planet. Through their faith, they most commonly believe in a spiritual Creator who promises life after death. In that perfect place, called "heaven," the promise is that they all will reside in peace at the side of our Lord God for eternity. Dwelling together therein will be all of their family, friends, and animals who shared their earthly life. They maintain the space by regularly attending a church, their house of God, temple, or mosque constructed according to the plans and peculiar philosophies inherited from their church and families. At first, as children, they are taught the basis for their faith and later, ritually confirmed into it. As the boy becomes a man, and the girl becomes a woman, their prayers and services for their God become routine, obligatory, and perfunctory.

In the Catholic faith of which I was confirmed, there is this thing called Confession. A confirmed Catholic will routinely go to confession which takes place in a confessional booth inside the church. The booth is constructed with a screened partition separating the confessor's identity from the priest. When the confessor completes his/her confession, the priest will command the confessor to a penance he feels suitable for forgiving the committed sins. It's a beautiful purification process where in the soul can regain a clean start and continue on to be a pure Christian practicing all the sacraments and the Ten Commandments. Upon death, the Christian then qualifies for entry into the Kingdom of Heaven. As time goes by and man gradually improves or worsens his condition and enjoys or is deprived of the plentiful fruits of life, the process of forgiveness for sins morphs into a thing called hypocrisy. Cause and effect of hypocrisy keep the wealth of doctors, drug companies, and psychiatrists in abundance to enjoy their own fruits of life.

In my opinion, when a human baby is expelled from the womb, the newly born infant immediately, with a pure infant heart, enters into the true "Third Temple," which is the permanent House of God. No steeple, building, concrete, bricks, or specially carved, gold doors constructed 10 blocks away from where you reside is required for your worship and support. Throughout the child's journey through life, temptation will be everywhere, while millions upon millions of religious worshipers and churches, temples, and mosques around the globe will wear out their knees and prayer for lighter burdens, while they fail to recognize and respect the physical magnificence of their God-given bodies' need for exercise to strengthen their backs to carry those burdens. For those wishing for lighter burdens, life on Earth may be the hell they fear. For the person who succeeds to walk among all mankind with God in his/her heart and accepts the power of doing good deeds, they are the ones who will contribute to a better world. Maybe this life is then the heaven we all seek? After all is said and done, with all of the poignant beauty of a moonlit night and warmth of a sunlit day, in those special moments we may experience, what then could be more heavenly? This is a quatrain from Omar Khayyam's Rubaiyat which I think gives some insight into the Persian poet's thoughts about tranquility or heaven on Earth:

"Here with a loaf of bread beneath the bough,

A flask of wine, a book of verse - and thou,

Beside me singing in the wilderness -

And wilderness is Paradise enow."

This is my vision of a perfect transition from this life on Earth to final placement in a heavenly paradise. Upon my death, during the viewing of my body Andrea Bocelli, Luciano Pavarotti, and Josh Groban in chorus will be singing "It's Time to Say Goodbye." Upon arrival in Heaven, everyone will be drifting on soft white clouds, cradled in the arms of our Father

God while listening to Enya's ethereal voice that will never end.

However, for all good and beauty of God's creation it's difficult to imagine the complete love of God, with all the beauty of this planet while it's eclipsed by the privilege inhabitants that God created, who intentionally torture and massacre their fellow man. Who are eclipsed by the greedy who failed to share their harvests with those who labor in their fields. When their dinner plates overflow with the fruits of plenty and poor children while looking on, watching through windows are cold and hungry. Wherein, on this planet of spectacular wealth, there are more tears from pain and suffering than there are of Joy from abundance. The ratio of poverty and hunger versus pain and joy begs the question, does pain and suffering qualify for eternal peace in heaven? Will those of great wealth who intentionally contribute to the suffering and condemnation of the helpless and disadvantaged be condemned to the fires of hell? Or will all the greedy, glutinous, devils of over consumption the forgiveness logic also be admitted into heaven, to dwell in the house of the Lord side by side with those who suffered in life?

In conclusion, there are no earthly answers known for the existence about all biological life forms on this planet. Certainly, no one has ever authentically come back from the dead and offered explanations for what is beyond life on earth. Again, the poet Omar Khayyam and his Rubaiyat expresses this well.

"There was a Door in which I found no key:

There was a Veil past which I could not see:

Some little Talk awhile of ME and THEE.

There seem'd - and then no more of THEE or ME."

Thank you, Omar!

Feeling Guilty?

Looking at an unfinished bone?
My pet dog at the age of eleven
Passed away quietly and went into doggie heaven.
Over there, where she sat with her sad eyes,
No longer greeting me with a waggin' tail,
And giving me her bashful doggie smile,
Too weak to finish her food and not knowing why,
Or understand that it was time to say goodbye,
Knowing the kind of love we'll never share again
With the loss of my loyal friend and then,
Someone, I don't remember who or when,
Said, "Maybe it's time
For you to have another new pooch." "Okay, fine!"
And so, the feeling of guilt slowly declined.
On my lap, an innocent head rests, a new friend of mine.
Argentinean Dogo, Sasha, in her new home
And has Skates's unfinished bone.
She now receives all the love I got and gave,
That didn't end in Skates's grace.
In the quiet earth where now rests the love
Of my old pal, Skate, which continues on

Now for my new furry friend.
So, now we all know it's okay to love again!
And for a new dog to finish the bone
Left behind in the other dog's home.

Bits & Pieces of an Ordinary Man's Life

A Shivering Chat

A fallen piece of a metal roof, a cardboard freight box.
Inside on this cold night, a homeless man falls asleep,
Little known by those of means who scorn, he once was a doc.
A scruffy old passerby, holding a half empty bottle of gin,
Taps on the roof, begging him to move over and let him in.
"It's cold out here, I'll share with you my gin!"
As it came to pass, being allowed inside, the two began to chat.
"How did you wind up this way?' inquired the new arriver.
"It's a long story, my friend, but you needn't worry,
There was a time when I hungered for fame and glory.
I had it all, the best of everything, respect, and dignity.
So, what I don't need now is your collaborative pity.
What, may I ask, is the ill fate in your life that led you here?"
"You may not believe it, sir, but I was a production engineer!
Like you, I had respect, and the pride of a worker's community.
I helped produce wonderful things in harmony and unity."
"So why is it that you lost everything you once had?"
"As it turns out those wonderful products that we once made,
Capitalists closed our plant, and they went to China to be made.
Incentives compensated corporations under the auspice of fair trade!

That's me! What about you, weren't you, a doctor and your own boss?"
"Insurance companies! Paperwork and untenable malpractice cost!
Insurance telling doctors how and what to prescribe,
Hospital corporations gradually took away our professional ability to decide!
Now, my homeless professional friend, where do we go from here?"
Until freedoms individual self-assertion isn't either by greed,
"We'll be joined by many millions of homeless, on sidewalks and streets,
Come from the poverty of small government will never be freed!
I don't know about you, I'm no longer a doctor drinking Scotch, I'd love a beer!"
"My reality, Doc, when nothing is being produced, who needs a production engineer?"
"Get some sleep, we'll need strength tomorrow to surf garbage cans,
Then we'll go to the beach, pretending we're different and get a tan!"

Merely a Man

In the morning, I stand in the Rising Sun.
I look long and study the growing grass.
It's so wonderful. Am I the one,
Who hears its sound and has a soul?
It's in my own silent music and tone.
The love of all, wondering if I am alone?
Maybe I would have been a better horse,
Or a dog whose scent knows where he hid the bone.
Tonight again, I'll gaze at the stars, of course.
They will be awesome, a powerful cosmic force.
And I'll wake again to what reality really means.
And discover, nothing of me is what I imagined it to be.
Wonder of wonders, I am what I am, so it would seem.
Tomorrow, I'll stand in the rising sun again,
Feel the warmth, hear the whispers of nature,
Armed with the truth that I'm merely a man,
Who is a star-struck, gazing creature.

Broken Wing

Alone on a leafless oak tree branch was perch the young sparrow,
Having a mother, but no father, was her Constant Sorrow,
Endowed with colorful plumage, she was ready to fly.
Although born with a damaged wing, she wanted to try.
Why mother, why, am I so broken, and unlike other birds, can't fly?
For every attempt failed and saddened her more when others flew.
The time to leave has passed, and her mama bird did too.
Alone in her nest, a tiny, feathered heart caps a rhythmic beat,
Searching all the trees in the forest and other nests,
In the hope of a father bird, she would finally meet.
If he soars like an eagle or has a broken wing like me,
If he loves me, I'll be happy, and with my love maybe,
We can both fly away from the branch of this old oak tree.

Where Are You, Daddy?

I need to know if it's true,

Am I me because of you?

There's an empty space in my heart.

What's keeping us apart?

I asked my mother, "Who is my real father, what's my real name?"

And she would always try to explain,

"You're just like your father, you're him, you're both the same!

Someday I'll tell you and hope you'll understand,

And then I'll tell you all that I can."

That someday oh, that someday, it never came.

My mother went to heaven before she could explain,

About my empty space and growing pain.

Young, lonely, and growing ever more sad,

I longed more than ever for the hand of my real dad.

Where are you, daddy? I Want to Hold Your Hand.

Where are you, daddy? I Want to Hold Your Hand.

In my dream, I see you, and struggle to see your face,

And wait for the day when you complete my empty space,

And if my dreams ever do come true,

I'll have what I've longed for is a daddy-dance with you.

Where are you, Daddy? I Want to Hold Your Hand.

Where are you, Daddy? I Want to Hold Your Hand.

I need to know who I am,

I need to know if it's true.

I'm me because of you.

Twin Emotions

What is it, that space which lies between Fidelity and infidelity?
Imagine all the ambiguous nuances of thought!
A place between being optimistic and being caught.
To move forward into an unknown future or shelter in the past?
In denial of a die that's already been cast.
A place where hope is in limbo, a place of Daring to Care,
A space where nothing is right or wrong,
A place you cannot remain too long.
visions of exclusive white and/or black in your song.
A place where lies never die, and you never hear the song.
A place in the darkness of Night, and the place you belong.
Who among all of us has ever been there?
The place where God has sent you, only to find the devil's Lair.
In the darkness of an empty room, nothing but you there,
Where words suddenly appeared in white, plain to see,
Your ecstasy has become the tragedy.

A Resting Place

Looking back at the past and place it to the rear at last,
You'll see a future Tranquility that's about to begin,
Which also means you must forgive every sin,
And all the mistakes you ever fully made.
Then, the sun will shine brighter as you move from the shade,
and embrace the ethereal chance of something new.
In this wonderful world that's waiting for me, too.
Out there, in a quiet place, for all of us, sans end,
And all of the poignant natural beauty it sends,
Where you and I will reside together forever,
To be resting on a new cloud of peace, together forever,
until the sun burns out and all the stars fall,
Out of the endless nocturnal dark sky,
Will catch the brightest one of all,
And ride past the moonshine until the end of time
Because it's wonderful new world of yours and mine
And, eventually, for all those in our orbit left behind.

Bits & Pieces of an Ordinary Man's Life

What's My Name?

From a stranger's breast I was fed,
Then left on the local church doorstep, I believe,
To be adopted by a couple who needed a child of their own,
Since the husband was sterile, having no seeds to be sown.
It was important, a baby they were unable to conceive!
in spite of their good intentions, prayers, and pleas,
Their ability to be parents sadly fell to the Wayside,
When suddenly the baron husband became ill and died.
Well, she mourned for a while before plotting her next move.
She powdered her face, perfumed her body, and got in the groove.
In time, she found her prey, a man with sperm intact.
While she was on the hunt, I was alone in a dirty shack.
So, as fate would have it, a new baby boy arrived.
He was celebrated with loving parents and was baptized.
With their new bubbly pride and joy,
My new role as an older stepsibling was set aside,
By a parent, whose fulfillment now had her own baby boy.
So, being accustomed as the unwanted child, once again alone.
I hit the streets in search of my own home.
It's weird, I was never baptized and given a name,
Or had my birth celebrated with caviar and champagne.

Alone is the way I departed the womb of Jane Doe,
Without knowing who I am. Seems likely the way I'll go.
"Drink up, Joe!"

Unexplained

He saw the sun and felt it's warm,

Watched it rise in the morning and go down at night.

The stars were also there, beautiful and bright.

Somewhere out there, dogs were barking at the moon.

Other planets exist, as witness through a telescope lens.

The sun, stars, and moon caused lovers to swoon.

As it was in the beginning of man, we can't pretend.

He emerged from his cave, searching for food on all fours,

Light years, centuries, decades becoming scores,

Evolved in time to an upright stance, learns to dance and dine.

On all the fruits of a planet spinning through time.

He came to understand how grapes could turn into wine.

He heard the Thunder, felt the Wind and Rain.

Not wanting to complain or appear insane,

He asked the clerics to explain about God because he cares.

The answers were always the same: "He's up there!"

What is it that he can't see, hear, feel, or touch?

Curious about the why does it bother him so much?

Canadian geese are honking in formative flight.

What then makes all biological forms so right?

Stupefied by his ignorant, pondering mind,

He knew it was time for him to unwind.
Never having seen, spoken to, or touched God,
The unshakable warmth of the sun, and its essence
Heard the voices of angels and feel their presence.
Isn't that odd?

The Heart of a Crow

If you think you have the character of a crow,
Perhaps these odd things you should know.
Just because a thing is yellow, doesn't mean it's gold.
High above you in a treetop, touching the dusky sky
Is where the black crows fly.
Its nest is loaded with shiny things and nothing of value.
He majestically scans the forest floor like a venerable statue,
Just like you, tracing in a pattern with your tantalizing eyes.
High above the fading sun, sit the Raven, bathing in the evening air.
Tomorrow, he'll fly without a care like the swishing of your black hair.
Just like the Flight of the ebony Bird high above thee,
Is your adorable soul searching for the answers of your mystery?
As you were more than once told of your Indian Heritage,
it would now seem appropriately so
That your heart identifies with the free flight of a crow.
Wherever in the height of the winter's snow,
or in the heat of the summer sun's glow,
The more he flies, the more you'll know,
About the aching emptiness in your own soul.

Just Thinking

Alone in my thoughts. Isn't everyone?
Nocturnally, daily on this planet and under the sun?
There's a boy-child off-key playing his father's guitar,
A girl sits at her window, cradling a doll, wishing on a star.
Soldier in his Foxhole during the darkest of nights
Wonders if he'll shoot when the enemy's in his sight.
A sailor who's sailing, dreams of his tomorrow's.
Will he be a plumber, doctor, or a lawyer?
And old man at life's end is peaking from his window,
Trying to avoid thoughts of when it will be his time to go.
Man as an oxygen consuming creature of this earth,
Will question all the whys as they search.
Alone, alone everyone from beginning to end,
Are thinking alone, as are their closest friends.
Often words cannot describe a thought,
Of life, love, death, or for the freedom we once fought.
Where and when do we start, and when will we eventually go,
Wondering if there is a God ends with a dismissive, "Who knows?"

As Clouds Pass

There sat by the ocean an artist whose passion exceeded the raging sea.
Upon his easel sat an empty canvas, waiting for his brush patiently.
This would be the moment, his need for exceptionalism was finally here.
He would paint the ocean's glory and power without fear.
The sky darkened, and raindrops reached the fresh paint, and it smeared.
As it began to appear to him, this may have been his best work this year!
There was a singer who sang love songs for all the world's lovers to hear,
Accompanied by a chorus of angels who echoed God's music from above.
Videos and radios played his music for all the beating hearts completely in love.
Yet, in his own soul, were the lyrics missed of what couldn't be replaced:
The real desire of seeing his father's approving face.

There was a dancer whose devotional need was to choreograph the ultimate motion,
To create human movement upon the dance floor, like waves in the ocean.
She danced and danced for hours, until her passion finally did subside.
Her painful, aching muscles gave her the solace of having tried,
Unable to produce the greatness of a dance. What was it she's trying to hide?
There was this poet whose rhythmic soul searches for words to explain
Man's passion of why the poignancy of all that's beautiful often leads to pain.

Blurred

Seems as though tomorrow is already yesterday.
That's how fast your time slips away.
It was a long time ago when I walked proudly along the beach,
Enjoying the wind on my dark hair and a comb within my reach.
Those years have passed by so fast.
I was young, handsome, undaunted, and strong, but nothing lasts.
Fertile mind, absolute conviction, fear I'd never feel,
Looking back, it seems as though it wasn't me! I wasn't real!
I was different, I was young, running and jumping every day.
The days were long then, and my tomorrows were far away.
And now tomorrow is already yesterday.
Something sweet in the mornings, opening of your sleepy eyes,
As another sun-filled day has signaled that you're still alive.
With the dark hair long gone and your unsteady gait,
Easing out of bed, no time to waste; What must be done can't wait.
Standing by the bed, wobbling, trying to refocus your vision,
While attempting to walk, you fall, forced to crawl. Bad decision!
A blurred tear falls, a sweet moment passed. It's too late!
The dogs are barking.

Ascending

Gently floating, spiritually floating, my angel is calling.
As of a white feather on a soft cloud, I am at peace.
That love song without words—the sounds of a waterfall,
Never silenced, always in my heart—is now released.
In this world of greed, jealousy, hatred, and lies,
Understanding why only in those rare acts of kindness,
Tenderness, and old movies did tears fill my eyes.
Finally, this thing we've come to know as human birth,
As residents is the only evidence of life on this earth.
The sun's warmth, moonlight magic, the stars bright
As jeweled blue diamonds, beautifying the darkest night.
Music, flowers, and animals beating in our hearts and souls
With such wonders that make our hearts grow.
In love, passion is a calling to leave our world a better place.
Upon this gentle cloud, there's no torture or pain. All is healed,
Left only to love and be loved and God's ethereal embrace.
Freely floating on this spiritual cloud is what I feel.
Leaving behind this place I love to the eternal love of above.
Never ending, never ending, never ending, being escorted by a dove.
Until I'm gone, gone from here, and then I never was.

Nothing ever was, no yesterdays or tomorrows, none of us.
Until a November day, I was here with you, then family.
And then to understand it's only the experience of being alive.
Where the air we breathe and pure water were needed to survive.
There's the only proof of a unique world's living community.
On this beautiful, soft cloud, I'm gently riding to the end,
Humbly grateful just the unsolved mystery of having been.
For all those whose love delivered my body, soul, and DNA,
Onto the universe of heaven and its eternal peace, I pray.
When there, I will wait for the softest and purest white cloud,
Laden with the voices of proud angels, whom by God we're allowed,
To deliver all the humans, cats, horses, and deer,
The beautiful things in my life will again be near.
Where all of us, free of hunger, hatred, and pain
Will in Heaven be together again.

Silly Old Guy

I'm up. I'm walking. I'm on my way.

I don't know where I'm going, but I'm going anyway.

If you think you understand, you'll get out of my way.

If in my direction and obstacles should cause me to fall,

Just help me up and lean me against the wall.

I'm up. I'm walking. I'm on my way, on my way.

Checked my eyes and limbs; it's the best I'll be all day.

There was this odd dream I had before I woke,

Free of aches and pain, relieved it wasn't a stroke!

There's no good rhyme, no reason, or why I even bother to try.

I guess I'm just one more silly old guy!

When everything is right, and nothing is wrong, it's just me.

If I don't get out at least once every day, I'm not free!

An Ocean of Tears

Every tear that falls from a man, woman, or child's eyes,
Journeys its way to the river of life, hoping to survive.
Into that river wherein memories of happiness and sadness dwell,
That body of water made up of all the tears that ever fell,
Carries a cargo of joy and sadness to the deep ocean of life.
All the waves grew higher and were tossing the ships at night.
Screamed to the stars and moon, "My load of sorrow has reached its height."
A thundering voice from the darkness calmed the angry waves,
Proclaiming, "Your depth is enough to carry all burdens. Be brave!"

Truth on the Hoof

The devil enters the scene, the reins of the white horse's bridle making a swishing sound.

He smiles as he looks at the prostrate people kneeling on the ground.

To his rear, a newborn fawn is fighting for its mother's nipple as a black cat saunters by.

And then, and then, he stopped, smiling as he heard a baby from a nearby stable cry.

"Can it be, can it really be," thought he. "Nah, never! I am the only ruler of this earth and planet there will ever be!"

The sky began to darken, and the wind became eerily still, all breathing of every creature all seemed to see the real deity.

The eyes of the horse widened with a look of horror upon his face as the devil's steadying attempt yanked hard on the rein.

It wasn't right; Lucifer was losing control, and his frozen face now displayed fear.

For the first time, he sensed a challenge, a pain.

The prostrate, kneeling crowd were cheering; the black cat, little fawn, and her mother were joined by others as toward the stable they trod.

All of their fears were about to end when they first would see baby Jesus, the Son of God.

Searching

At times, I feel like a three-dimensional cloud, floating over the forest.
Searching for my heart and soul, while nowhere are they to be found.
And I awake from the dream,
In the dream at intervals the sun would cast my empty shadow upon the ground.
Whereas the sight of running Bambi could be seen.
And this would be a sign, the beginning of my love for wild things.
In the light of day, in the shape of a human being, I begin to sing.
Love songs, love songs, in ethereal sounds.
As the day lengthens, it's a reality. My heart and soul were never found.
A corpus in appearance with a large hole wherein a heart should be located.
Searches in dreams for the reason it was vacated.
Tonight, I'll sleep and wait for another dream to end my sorrow.
And walk proudly away from a park bench hosting a better tomorrow.
In passing, my image is seen in a mirror on the wall.
The shadow has shown age and will do more in the fall.

Oh, well, Bambi's adorable eyes will fill the empty space this year.

And the scent of lily of the valley will shed more tears.

In walking away, Bambi's head cradles my arm, signaling a pure love that will never be harmed.

Today Is Mine; Tomorrow Is Yours

Be warmed by the sun and shine with the stars.
Be happy every day, go for a drive in your new car.
Don't worry about tomorrow or waste any time with sorrow.
When you're gone, new life in the world will go on.

Be warmed by the sun and shine with the stars.
Stop howling at the moon and wishing on Mars.
Run like a horse, feel the rhythm in your heart, to you it belongs.
When you're gone, new life in the world will go on.

Be warmed by the sun and love the night.
Reach out, give a hand up to a fellow man; it's right.
On your deck, shrouded in darkness, reminiscing of a beautiful day.
When you're gone, new life and the world will go on; it's God's way.

Be warmed by the sun, but welcome the rain.
Fly high into the clouds, holding onto the Pegasus rein.

Smell the sweet scent of life, again and again.
When you're gone, life will go on sans end.

Be warmed by the sun and feel all what's real.
Sing love songs all day long, smell a perfume ethereal.
Don't be exclusive with your friends, White or Black
When you're gone, life goes on, and you're not coming back.

Be warmed by the sun and shaded by all the trees.
Love the disadvantaged and help the blind to see.
Forget about getting; giving will set you free.
When you're gone, life will go on without you or me.

I'm warmed by the sun; I bathe in the colors of love.
I feel the blueness of a blue jay and the purity of a dove.
I sing the songs of angels, loud and clear.
They pretend not to see or hear, but I'm still here.

I'm warmed by the sun and feel life sans fear.
I sing some songs in silence that only my heart can hear.
This moment, this park bench, is forever dear.
When we're gone, those who follow will know we were here.

Be warmed by the sun, love all who you can, love everyone.

Love the color of Monday as much as Saturday.

Be content within your soul and in your heart say,

Let today be mine; it's fate. Tomorrow is yours; have fun.

The Non-Organ

There was this mysterious, odd pain.
It wasn't a big place that was hard to explain.
I felt childish and guilty when at the doctor's I'd complain.
He looked at me in a dubious way and said, "Let's see!
On a scale of 1 to 10, where would it be?"
"It's a mild sensation when I'm walking about,
And it's nowhere on that scale you're talkin' about!"
"Well, where and when are you experiencing the pain,
This pain can you tell me, how Intense or explain?"
"Doc, it comes, and it goes. Most of the time, I'm fine.
However, the intervals seemed to last a very long time."
"As far as science has shown of every cell, muscle, and bone,
We practitioners can't possibly or never have acted alone.
Young man, let's run some tests, but I think I already know,
It's not your heart, lungs, or organs the tests will show.
Only God knows where you'll find your soul!"

Bits & Pieces of an Ordinary Man's Life

The Neighborhood

I have set my feet upon many glorious streets, from my hometown to the famous streets of many foreign lands. In Paris, I sensed its class struggles. In Spain, I observed the language of love. In France, I borrowed a bit of their culture, while in Rio De Janeiro, Brazil, I touched the feet of a Christ the Savior statue and felt the welcome of outstretched hands. In Portugal, I visited Fatima on a dreary, overcast day and left feeling conflicted. Having seen some of the most amazing endeavors of man, every step that I made was set upon innocently and without a plan. Yes, every moment, every step I took was with an open boy's heart, laden with memories of where I came from.

That street as short as it was, had this common name, Mine Street. It was so named because most of the men living on Mine Street worked in the anthracite coal mines. In my heart and soul, it is the one street I'm always on, a street that never ends. The street, when entered from the bottom of our block, is where BooBee's Salon hosted an after-work crowd of neighborhood workers and friends. This street where I'm from tells you who I am and until death will always be, a black-soot-faced guy scrubbed clean.

Always within my reoccurring thoughts, I see my father and his rolled-up short sleeves walking toward our home, but he never gets there. It's always summer in my memory of him. He never ages, nor do I ever see him wearing a coat or jacket. It's only his tanned, muscular arms I ever see. When I say walking, there were times when he was staggering from BooBee's. This is what hard-working men did when they didn't have cars. There was no such thing as "driving under the influence" back then.

At times, more than one man could be seen staggering drunk up Mine Street to get home from BooBee's. They staggered home on foot, and I guess it could be punishable today as an intoxicated ambulatory offense. But who cared?

There were days when being an American meant you really were free. If you smoke cigarettes, it was *your* funeral. If you were drunk, it was *your* family who suffered, and nobody went to jail.

Mine Street was paved with macadam from Mill to Hill Street. Black macadam ended at the foot of a very short hill, where it turned to dirt—a short, steep hill with a dirty, dirt road. On the north side of the road was the last of the four in-row company houses on Mine Street.

Across the street, the southside of Mine Street was open field were all the kids played. Sometimes, an open trash fire would be burning there for days, where people in the neighborhood would share in the control. We kids would steal potatoes from grandmas and roast them on the fire. Actually, as I recall, the black, charcoaled skin was as delicious as a steaming, white potato waiting for our hungry stomachs.

Living within these four in-row homes, the homogenized American culture truly existed. As a mixed Italian/German family, we Fazios lived. It was the last end home at 545 East Mine Street. Living next door down 543, was a German family the Stoekels, who are my uncles, aunts, and maternal grandparents. Continuing down at 541 lived the Marleys, an Irish family, and in the last home of the company row homes at 539, East Mine Street, lived the Pini family. They were of Tyrolean descent.

On Sundays, the Fazios went to the Holy Rosary Church, the Stoekels went to a German Protestant church, Marleys to Saint Gabriel's, an Irish Catholic church, and finally the Pinis worshipped at the Lady of Mount Carmel, which was a Tyrolean church. All of the four, different-cultured families found a way to worship the same God in slightly different religious ways, raise their children in the moment, and eat each other's pizza, meat, and potatoes, and sauerkraut. That was the America I was socialized into as a kid.

The Pinis at 539 were interesting. Two cousins from the same village in Tyrol had immigrated to America around the same time. The cousin Augustus Pinis became the landlord of the four in-row homes. They went to the same church in Tyrol. In America, they went to the same church in Hazleton, Pennsylvania, Our Lady of Mount Carmel. Ironically, the priest from their church in Tyrol also came to America and became their priest here.

Mr. Pini, I don't know much about. But his two sons and daughter were among all the neighborhood children who we played with. His daughter was my age, and looking back, I guess she was my first friend, but that's a story for another time.

So, what's my point? My point is, no matter where I've been bits and pieces of France, Germany, Spain, Portugal, Brazil, and islands in between are in my heart with me on Mine Street!

Retired

Speaker, sir, for whom do you speak?
Is it for the strong or coming from an inner voice you need to repeat?
What is it that I heard you say?
Clouds don't sing, and the sun doesn't shine in the grave. Or do they?
You can't live in the past; nothing lasts anyway!
Is life always about tomorrow but not today, is what you say.
Well, my friend,
When all the work ends, it becomes only about yesterday.
Dreamers, dream on, and let your sweet nights never end.
Workers, work hard and work harder every day.
Friend, be a friend and give but never ever lend.
Singer, open your heart to the lyrics you pray.
Listener, listen more and listen well to what you hear.
Music heard is a soothing guide from every there to everywhere.
Steps you take, take with caution to avoid hell and never tell.
Do everything you need to do and never hide.
When your journey ends, your heart and soul will be calm.
Then go eagerly and enter the ethereal clouds with pride.
And hear the angles sing the Twenty-Third Psalm.

Retirement is the period between purpose and being gone.

Only between riverbanks does all water flow.

A life remembered is but a small pond.

Just for Awhile

From the dark void and into the light
Is the mystery of what becomes our life.
The essence of everything that is and ever will be—
For a while, just a little while, a family, a wife—
Is why God made you and me.
And in that while, we see all the wonders and whys,
Of green grass and white, soft pillow clouds,
Gently making love to a never-ending blue sky.
Crows crowing, seagulls pleasing the beach crowd,
Cardinals and blue jays and graceful light
And all the other living, glowing eyes.
Our privilege to view a breathtaking moon at night,
admiration, and joyous smiles.
All living beings during this precious while.
As mothers and fathers love to feel,
Descends taste and touch upon everything real.
These two emotions of love and hate,
Known by some as Kismet or Fate.
Then we seem to realize, everything will end.
Sleep is forever, not just a while. Why pretend?
The wisest thing isn't crossing T's or dotting I's.

It's living and doing well without questioning why!
Nothing is known of the world beyond,
Until then, in this wonderful world for a while
Now's the time to kiss your dad and mom,
And learn to smile.

Alone

Long dead are the old acquaintances and friends.
Being old and getting older, being closer to the end.
Stories no one wants to hear repeated,
None of which today are useful or needed.
Maybe having another brandy will do?
Listening to old music is better than hearing you.
All those streets you walked upon before,
Are gone; they don't exist anymore.
So, you see, your walks down memory lane,
Will be alone, soon forgotten is your name.
So, have no fear; it happens, so don't pretend.
The ride is close to the end.

A Friend Flew In

In my early twenties, I owned a 1954 two-tone Chevrolet. The roof was white, and the lower body was blue. Although I was living in Weatherly, Pennsylvania, at the time, I was working as a shipping clerk in a slipper factory in Hazleton, Pennsylvania. The price of gasoline averaged under $0.50 a gallon, which made the 20-mile round trip commute to work affordable.

Anyway, with that description of my white-top Chevy etched in your mind, while approaching my home several blocks away, a beautiful, black crow landed on the roof of my car and rode the rest of the way home with me. It became a daily habit with the crow welcoming me home. The crow and I became friends.

He wasn't just a fluky crow. He was a comedian who would play taunting games with me. One day, I was doing something with my side lawn and had my open pack of Pall Mall cigarettes lying on the grass. Joe the crow (the name I gave him) pulled a cigarette out of the pack and began running around with it in his beak while I was chasing him around for the cigarette. Joe was really enjoying himself as I was hysterically trying to catch him.

Joe had his nest somewhere in a neighborhood tree, which I was never able to locate. He belonged to the skies, and with his God-given eyes, he decided to pick me as his human friend. In general, at the time, my life was unsettled, but Joe made me happy.

One sunny, warm day, as I was washing my car, Joe came from out of nowhere and decided to pay me a visit. He landed on my white roof, and because it was still wet, he slid off like in a Road Runner cartoon

My days weren't complete without some interaction with Joe the crow.

Sadly, one day passed when I didn't see Joe. As days turned into weeks without seeing my black-feathered friend, I finally had to accept the truth that it was over. My rare, comedic relationship with a crow was finished.

Ever since Joe, I have admired and developed a lifelong love for crows. When Joe suddenly disappeared, although the crow brought pleasure into my unsettled life, and as much of a joy it was for me, it must have been an annoyance to other mindless opportunists who enjoy shooting birds. What Joe the innocent, friendly crow didn't even know is that not all humans can be trusted.

Ever wonder why at times you see people with facial features that resemble those of a bird? I do, but in the most beautiful way. When I say, "You remind me of a crow," it really means I like you, and somehow you brighten up my otherwise dark place.

The End!

Bits & Pieces of an Ordinary Man's Life

About the Author

I am a high school dropout. I finished my GED, and I attended the Military Police Training Academy, which was at Fort Gordon, Georgia.

I started taking college courses on the Army base in France, through the University of Maryland. I received a certificate in personnel management from King's College, in Wilkes-Barre, Pennsylvania. I graduated from the Pennsylvania Department of Corrections Academy.

Throughout my life, I worked in various heavy industries and jobs, including for a slipper/shoe factory, a trailer manufacturer, a steel manufacturer, and a correctional facility. I also owned a tavern. I went to school at the Hazleton State General Hospital for two years to become certified as a supportive physical therapist. Then I worked for years as a supportive physical therapist, which I loved because it gave me the opportunity to help people.

I served on the advisory boards of the Hazleton Chapters of the American Heart Association and of the Arthritis Foundation. I also served as the Arthritis Foundation Hazleton Chapter board president. I served as well on the board of governors of the Hazleton Art League. For our local Veterans of

Foreign Wars (VFW) Post 8225, I was Vice Commander and Commander for several terms. I was named Aide-de-Camp for the national VFW because of our success maintaining 100 percent reenrollment in our post.

I'm also the author of *Final Duty*.

I am a proud American who served my country in the U.S. Army. As a civilian, I was an elected Borough Mayor, and I served three terms—12 years.

Today, I live in Albrightsville, Pennsylvania, with my wife, Christine, and our dog, Sasha.

Politically, I am Socially Progressive but Fiscally Conservative, which I believe classifies me as a Moderate.

People perfunctorily say, "Thank you for your service."

"It was an honor for me to serve in both capacities," I usually reply. Serving my country did more for me than I could ever do to repay it, considering all the sacrifices our forefathers made for me to live freely in our Democracy.

An American flag proudly flies in front of my home throughout the year. Inside my home is a pocket copy of the U.S. Constitution.

I love my family, community, and country, and I want a free, meaningful, prosperous life for all of them.

In this one life we have been privileged to experience, in a nation dedicated to equal rights, may the bits and pieces of your life's journey be as rewarding for you as they have been for me.

www.ingramcontent.com/pod-product-compliance
Lightning Source LLC
Chambersburg PA
CBHW042112120526
44592CB00042B/2708